It was Fifty Years Ago today
THE BEATLES Invade America and Hollywood

by Harvey Kubernik

Front cover photo courtesy of "The Ed Sullivan Show" photos (c) SOFA Entertainment, All Rights Reserved (http://www.edsullivan.com).

Back cover items courtesy of Ray Randolph, Harvey Kubernik Archives, Gary Pig Gold Archives and Charlene Nowak.

David Leaf quotes copyright DLP 2013.

All appropriate lengths were taken to secure proper photo credits and permissions as well as attribution of quotes to editorial voices. Any omissions or errors are deeply regretted and will be rectified upon reprint.

This book became a distributed retail document owing partially to the spiritual, financial, supportive combined efforts of Carol Schofield, Kathie Zeigler, MsMusic Productions , along with the karmic guidance of S. Ti Muntarbhorn, in association with Harvey Kubernik.

Om Mani Padme Hum

It was Fifty Years Ago Today

THE BEATLES Invade America and Hollywood

by Harvey Kubernik

Otherworld Cottage Industries
Los Angeles

First Printing, February 2014

© 2014 by Harvey Kubernik

All rights reserved, including the right to reproduce this book or any portion thereof in any form, without the written permission of the Author, except that a reviewer may quote and a magazine or newspaper may print brief passages as part of a review written specifically for inclusion in that magazine or newspaper. For further information, email travpike@morningstone.com.

Kubernik, Harvey
It Was 50 Years Ago Today: The Beatles Invade America and Hollywood

1. Beatles 2. Beatles--History 3. Rock Musicians--England--Biography
I. Harvey Kubernik. II. Title. III. Title: The Beatles Invade America and Hollywood

782.421

ISBN-13: 978-0-9898936-8-8
ISBN-10: 0989893685

Printed in the United States of America
COPY EDITING: JOSEPH MCCOMBS
PHOTO AND ARTIFACT COORDINATION: HARVEY KUBERNIK AND GARY STROBL
FRONT COVER CONCEPT AND DESIGN: HEATHER HARRIS
BOOK COVER: LINDA SNYDER
BOOK LAYOUT AND DESIGN BY TRAVIS PIKE

DEDICATION

For Derek Taylor -- who loved the Beatles and really dug Hollywood. Photo by Jim Dickson/Henry Diltz Archives

TABLE OF CONTENTS

ix.   **FOREWORD BY JAMES CUSHING**

xiii. **PROLOGUE BY HARVEY KUBERNIK**

PART 1: NICK OF TIME   1

PART 2: LAST SECOND OF A BIG DREAM   71

PART 3: PRICK UP YOUR EARS   117

PART 4: SAVE THE TIGER   171

EPILIOGUE   217

ACKNOWLEDGMENTS   219

ABOUT THE AUTHOR   221

FOREWORD BY JAMES CUSHING

The Beatles and the Inner Life of Los Angeles, 1964–69,

Hollywood and the Beatles were the two greatest romances of the 20th century. What did they have in common? How did they intersect? How did one of these great affairs learn from the other?

Harvey Kubernik has posed himself these questions in this book and tried to answer them in the best way he knows: with the testimony of eyewitnesses, participants in a cultural history whose memory can no longer be taken for granted.

As American listeners, Harvey Kubernik and I came to the Beatles' sound-world from opposite coasts. I was a 10-year-old in the New York bedroom community of Westport, Connecticut, when the one-two punch of Dallas 11/22/63 and Ed Sullivan 2/9/64 alerted me to the terror and wonderment of the outside world. After those snowy days, I was no longer a little kid. I got excited about the first Beatles LP in a way I had never felt about my childhood favorites, the rousing Kingston Trio and the hilarious Stan Freberg. But I was still enough of a child to see what struck me as a key connection: the Trio and Freberg and the Beatles were all on the Capitol label, the one with the color spectrum around the rim, hypnotic as it rotated on my turntable, and these artists I loved were part of that beautiful Capitol color spectrum.

All I knew about Capitol was that it was located in Hollywood, as far away from Westport as Liverpool yet already familiar from the movies, Disneyland, and the future its designers spread across the country. To a 10-year-old staring at *Meet the Beatles!* as snow fell outside his bedroom window, the scene's meaning was clear: Los Angeles was where the colorful music came from.

The Beatles' colorful history in Los Angeles soon entered myth. The Hollywood Bowl concerts, George's "blessing" of the photographer at the Whisky a Go Go, the meeting with Elvis in Bel-Air, the mutual admiration/rivalry with that other Capitol records singing group whose name began with B-E-A – New York might have had the Brill Building, but L.A. had the sunshine and the new energy.

By the time I turned 13, in 1967, I was living in Coldwater Canyon, and L.A. stations played whole sides of *Sgt. Pepper*; rumors had George Harrison holed up somewhere in the Hollywood hills while the rest of the Beatles were making their own movie in London. That Christmas, Capitol released the deluxe version of *Magical Mystery Tour*, the Beatles' place-name album, with songs named after two locations in Liverpool (Strawberry Fields, Penny Lane) and a little cul-de-sac near Mulholland, "Blue Jay Way."

A year later, in November 1968, I first heard the *White Album* all the way through on KPPC radio, introduced by the composer of "Blue Jay Way." A Beatle had come to an "underground" hippie FM radio station in L.A. to preview the band's major work!

By 1969, I was a junior at the bad old all-male-military Harvard School and had struck up a friendship with a fellow music freak, a senior named John Gilmore. I stayed pretty calm when I learned that John's father was Voyle Gilmore, the man who had produced Frank Sinatra and all those Kingston Trio LPs I had worn out as a child. When John added that "my dad also produced a live Beatles album that never came out," I had to figure out a way to meet my friend's ultra-cool parents. Early in 1970, I wangled an invitation to a party at the Gilmores' and, I'm afraid, interrogated the kindly Mr. Gilmore about that Beatles album.

"It was actually two albums," he replied. "We recorded the Beatles at the Hollywood Bowl in 1964 and again in '65, but the noise from those screaming girls was just... It was like a whole airport worth of jet engines with a band playing in the background. And all the songs they did were familiar already from the records, so they decided to pass." Gilmore shrugged. "I have the acetates of both concerts if you want to listen to them, but they're pretty bad."

Like most civilians, I had never held an acetate disc in my hands. These were the same size as normal LPs, but stiffer, since they were made of aluminum with a thin acetate coating on which the groove was stamped. The labels had been typed in all caps, with THE BEATLES – HOLLYWOOD BOWL AUG. 1964 or AUG. 1965, and the listing of the songs. Light glinted off the acetate plastic in an eerie purple. I placed Side One of 1964 on the Gilmore's MacIntosh system, threaded the blank tape I had snuck into the house (just in case) onto their reel-to-reel, and understood that I was doing something deceptive but not wrong, that I loved this music this much, and I would never sell this tape I was making of these concerts, the more recent one already five years gone.

In 1977, a single LP compilation of those recordings was released, by Capitol, as *The Beatles at the Hollywood Bowl*. Voyle Gilmore was listed as producer. By then, John Lennon had moved to Los Angeles, liked it too much, and returned to New York to retire. Paul, George, and Ringo were already recording here; all of them would purchase homes in Los Angeles County; George would die in Los Angeles at 58, in 2001.

The Los Angeles connection continues to emerge and guide those touched by this music, this moment. I drive past Paul's house every now and then, and say an agnostic's prayer: "May the spirit and beauty of the Beatles never perish from the earth."

James Cushing
Los Angeles, California

(Dr. James Cushing (Ph.D. UC Irvine) has been teaching literature and creative writing at Cal Poly in San Luis Obispo since 1989. He regularly broadcasts jazz and rock programs on the college station, KCPR, 91.3FM (www.kcpr.org). He was SLO Poet Laureate from 2008-2010. His most recent collections are Pinocchio's Revolution (2009) and The Once-Familiar Shore (2014), both from Cahuenga Press in Los Angeles).

PROLOGUE BY HARVEY KUBERNIK

In 1974, I tried to write, let alone get published, an article about the Beatles and the 10-year anniversary of their arrival in the United States.

I first thought of the concept at George Harrison's 1974 Beverly Wilshire Hotel press conference on Wilshire Boulevard in Beverly Hills, where 10 years earlier I had seen, just down the same street, the February 1964 live Beatles, Beach Boys and Lesley Gore concert in a closed-circuit theatrical movie-house showing at the Fox Wilshire Theater.

I always thought and felt a local newspaper, or English music magazine might want to have an article on this unique rock 'n' roll band that made the magical 10-year mark. A story where I could say something about the Beatles' landing in America and the well-established ties to my Los Angeles–area West Hollywood hometown.

The Beatles' still ongoing and always expanding stateside impact went beyond their debut on *The Ed Sullivan Show*. That television appearance hurled the music at us. Then their moment on the L.A.–filmed and Jimmy O'Neill-hosted *Shindig!* ABC-TV series further cemented a telegenic and sonic legacy.

Wasn't their domestic record company located in Hollywood? How many local and national radio exclusives, distribution and sales machinations on their behalf were hatched at the 13-story Welton Becket–designed Capitol Records building on Vine Street near Hollywood Boulevard?

ABC TELEVISION NETWORK / 4151 PROSPECT AVENUE / HOLLYWOOD 27, CALIF.

September 17, 1964

THE BEATLES MAKE THE "SHINDIG" SCENE OCT. 7

The Beatles head a stellar lineup that includes seven of Britain's other top music talents, on "Shindig" Wednesday, Oct. 7 (ABC-TV, 8:30-9 PM, PDT).

According to "Shindig" producer Jack Good, en route to London to tape show segments, the famous foursome -- John Lennon, Paul McCartney, George Hamilton and Ringo -- will probably do four numbers on the program and perform with the other entertainers.

Also appearing on the program will be Cilla Blacke, 21, Liverpool's "Queen of the Mods" (short for Moderns) in her American TV debut. A former coffeehouse waitress discovered by the Beatles' manager, Brian Epstein, Cilla's hit record is "U're My World."

Sounds, Inc., an instrumental group from the south of England that recorded the theme music for the film, "The Spartans," will also appear. The sextet, comprised of a drummer, two guitarists, a pianist on the electric piano and two saxophonists, one of whom alternates on the flute, recently recorded "Spanish Harlem."

Other talent for the "Shindig" show will be signed after Good's arrival in London, where he produced an hour-long special, "Around the Beatles," last May.

- abc-tv -

Press release of September 17, 1964 courtesy of Jim Roup

Thankfully, during 40 years of published musical journalism, I would, on occasion, ask my interview subjects, songwriters, recording and mastering engineers, poets, multi-instrumentalists, graphic artists, philosophers, record producers, disc jockeys, authors, filmmakers, pen pals, photographers, and collectors about their timeless catalog and the influence of their very rarely chronicled-at-length history with Southern California and Hollywood.

In 2004 *Goldmine* magazine was planning a salute to the Beatles in its annual tribute issue. The editor contacted me, and wanted something new and different about the Beatles in America, and did I have a West Coast or L.A. childhood memory of the band?

I had 30,000 words sitting in my computer, and *Goldmine* printed a few thousand of them, my first-person memoir as centerpiece.

I received some cool fan letters and accolades from truly passionate and totally hardcore Beatle fans.

Later, the October 16, 2005, commemorative 100th anniversary issue of *VARIETY* magazine headlined the Beatles as the Entertainers of the Century in a commissioned cover profile, "Here There & Everywhere," written by my brother, fellow author Kenneth Kubernik.

During the fall of 2013, while simultaneously preparing for the publication of a few large format hardcover books for 2014, I realized the 50th anniversary of the Beatles' U.S. marketplace domination would be a media event and a forum for a celebration to be rolled out in February 2014. And, like their work, would continue for many years.

I sent out to a handful of music magazines and newspapers a rough draft of my existing 30,000 words, cobbled together in a neo-narrative word salad, partially drawn from taped interviews that weren't printed, never before heard voices, edited articles previously published in truncated fashion over the last 20 years in *HITS, Goldmine, treats!, WAVES!, MOJO* and *RECORD COLLECTOR news.*

A receptive executive editor, Steven Gaydos, at the Wilshire Boulevard–based *VARIETY* magazine first called and emailed. "Is some of this still available?" "Yes." "We'd like to run a piece of it in our September issue that will be celebrating 50 years of British Airways and 10 Brits to Watch."

When just a very small portion hit in a *VARIETY* three-page center spread titled "The Original Brits to Watch," after a front cover banner heralded "Ticket to Ride 50 Years of Fab Four," all sorts of wonderful phone calls and groovy emails came in from all over the world.

Many messages resulting from my *VARIETY* byline had the same recurring concern: "We really never read anything about the Beatles and their vital connection to Los Angeles and Hollywood."

This is a topic that we all collectively felt has been underserved.

So, I decided to do additional research and more writing on my four royal subjects, while assembling a global multiple-voice team report for this book, initially encouraged by poet/actor Harry E. Northup, who mandated an obligation to bring my information and prose "from private to public," and Buddhist S. Ti Muntarbhorn, requesting that I needed to "reveal this hidden, forgotten and never really documented extraordinary world."

On December 1, 2013, I was invited to attend and given an all-access pass to the 82nd Annual Hollywood Christmas Parade presented by Associated Television International. It benefited Toys for Tots and Disabled American Veterans.

I hadn't been at the Hollywood Christmas Parade in a half a century.

I walked on the red carpet that covered Hollywood Boulevard, albeit at the sound check for Stevie Wonder's spot at the televised event.

I was very delighted to nosh at the buffet in the Green Room, hear a pre-show band, and happy to talk to an original *Twilight Zone* actor, a cute network television actress, four publicists, three talent agents, two movie producers, and a show runner.

At the reception I said hello to astronaut Buzz Aldrin, who was the 2013 Grand Marshal.

This is the man who walked on the moon with Neil Armstrong in 1969.

So at least with this book I tried to hit the moon.

And in the process became a "Paperback Writer."

Harvey Kubernik
Hollywood, California

It was Fifty Years Ago today
THE BEATLES Invade America and Hollywood

by Harvey Kubernik

It Was 50 Years Ago Today: The Beatles Invade America and Hollywood

Jack Parr photo courtesy of Universal Media, Inc.

PART 1: NICK OF TIME

I was age 12, on the edge of 13, when the Beatles came to America in February 1964.

In mid-December 1963, Capitol Records rush-released "I Want to Hold Your Hand" after a stateside airplay on a Washington, D.C., radio station.

In Los Angeles, I had seen and heard the Beatles mentioned in a Walter Cronkite CBS news television program in December 1963 and their actual debut on American TV on January 3, 1964, when a segment ran on them on *The Jack Paar Program*. It was a grainy black-and-white clip of them performing "From Me To You" and "She Loves You" live. Paar told his viewers the Beatles were going to next appear on *The Ed Sullivan Show* the following month.

The New York–based Ed Sullivan was best known for his influential television hosting duties of the 1950s and 1960s, but before the small-screen exposure, he had been a newspaper columnist and show business personality beginning in the early '30s. He presented more than 10,000 performers over his prime-time TV career. He also portrayed himself in the movie *Bye, Bye Birdie.*

The Sunday night variety show, which ran from 1948 to 1971, was seen live in the Central and Eastern time zones but fortunately was taped for airing in the Pacific and Mountain time zones.

Sullivan initially became aware of the Beatles in 1963 at an airport. He swiftly arranged a meeting with their manager, Brian Epstein.

On November 5, 1963, immediately following the band's historic Royal Command Performance, Epstein flew to New York with Billy J. Kramer in order to huddle with the all-important editor of *16* Magazine, Gloria Stavers, as well as apply pressure to the American division of the EMI label, Capitol Records. On his trek to America, Brian visited Ed Sullivan as well to negotiate the Beatles' first booking on his show.

At first, Sullivan offered Epstein and the Beatles only a spot during one broadcast. Epstein, who had a 25% fee on Beatles income, stemming from an October 1962–1967 management contract, offered to pay travel, lodging and expenses, after Sullivan initially declined a headline appearance. Then Epstein countered with a guarantee for two different headline band appearances.

Sullivan was a bit miffed by Epstein's stern management demands. They settled on the two principal bookings, and then filmed another performance around the two appearances in Miami, which was put in the can and later shown as a third Beatles' booking on his popular series. Epstein was then able to use this secured national TV clout as leverage to force Capitol to spend a $50,000 promotional budget on his group, a figure never used for an unheard British musical import.

On February 7, 1964, The Beatles arrived at New York's John F. Kennedy Airport, greeted by scores of screaming, swooning fans who rushed the gate to catch a glimpse of John Lennon, Paul McCartney, George Harrison and Ringo Starr as they took their first steps on American soil.

Technically, George had been over to visit his sister Louise Harrison Caldwell in Benton, Illinois for a couple of weeks during September of 1963. Harrison purchased his first Rickenbacker guitar there, visited local AM station WFRX with a Parlophone 45 of "She Loves You," and even played a couple of sets with a local band.

George and his brother Peter (who was along for the trip; Ringo declined the invite) also spent a couple of days in New York City en route back to London.

When the Beatles stepped onto Ed Sullivan's New York stage on Sunday, February 9, 1964, to make their American TV debut, 86% of all TVs on at that hour—74 million Americans and millions more in Canada—were tuned in. It was the most watched program in history to that point and remains one of the most watched programs of all time.

Ed Sullivan spoke of the unprecedented frenzy in his memorable first introduction of the Beatles, saying, "Now, yesterday and today our theater's been jammed with newspapermen and hundreds of photographers from all over the nation, and these veterans agreed with me that this city never has witnessed the excitement stirred by these youngsters from Liverpool who call themselves the Beatles."

Ed also cited America's biggest star of the day, Elvis Presley, who along with his manager, Col. Tom Parker, sent the Beatles a telegram wishing them well for their national television debut.

To some, it will always be remembered by Sullivan's introduction: "Here they are—the Beatles!"

After the very first Beatles segment aired, Ed Sullivan told his studio audience and TV viewers, "Those first three songs went out to Johnny Carson, Randy Paar [Jack's daughter], and [newspaper columnist] Earl Wilson."

In this cultural watershed moment in American history and one of the world's top-viewed television events of all time, the Beatles did five songs on the live broadcast. "Beatlemania," already in full, feverish bloom in the Beatles' native U.K., was unleashed with blissful fervor across America and around the world. The British Invasion had begun.

**Watching The Beatles on The Ed Sullivan Show.
Photo by Rodney Bingenheimer, Mountain View, California**

The Beatles would appear live on *Sullivan* three more times: the following Sunday from Miami, a third consecutive show on February 23, and finally on September 12, 1965.

**Watching The Beatles on The Ed Sullivan Show.
Photo by Rodney Bingenheimer, Mountain View, California**

In all, the Fab Four performed 20 songs (15 different ones), from "All My Loving" and "I Saw Her Standing There" (twice each) to "I Want to Hold Your Hand" (three times), "Yesterday" and "Help!"

After captivating North America with their Ed Sullivan debut, The Beatles traveled to Washington, DC, performing their first Stateside concert on February 11 at the Washington Coliseum to 8,000 fans in the round. The Beatles then returned to New York for two sold-out Carnegie Hall concerts on February 12.

On February 16, they made their second appearance on *The Ed Sullivan Show* in a live broadcast from The Deauville Hotel in Miami Beach, Florida. Viewership for the episode was nearly as strong as for their debut one week prior, with an estimated 70 million people -- 40% of the American population -- tuned in to watch their performances of six songs. On February 22, The Beatles returned to England in triumph, welcomed home upon their 7am landing at London's Heathrow Airport by an estimated 10,000 fans.

The Beatles were now firmly in place as the world's favorite and most famous band. Their third *Ed Sullivan Show* appearance, a three-song performance taped prior to the band's live debut on the program, was broadcast on February 23. *Billboard's* Hot 100 Singles chart for April 5, 1964 was graced by 12 Beatles songs, including the chart's Top 5 positions, a sweep of the chart's summit that has not been achieved by any other artist since.

Nearly 50 years after the four landmark live performances of the Beatles on *The Ed Sullivan Show,* those groundbreaking appearances were finally made available worldwide in September 2010 on home video, with newly remastered audio and carefully restored video, through Universal Music Enterprises (UME) and produced by SOFA

Entertainment, which purchased all 1,050 hours of *The Ed Sullivan Show* in 1990.

"We used the full extent of today's technology," explained Andrew Solt, executive producer and CEO of SOFA Entertainment, from his West Hollywood Sunset Boulevard offices. "The quality is better than it ever was, in fact, better than when the shows aired, especially visually.

Few tapes had been transferred to a contemporary format until Solt obtained the rights. Today he continues to transfer and remaster them.

"Usually when there is a major historic moment, it's seen on every channel," remarked Solt. "What makes the first Beatles performance so unusual is that *The Ed Sullivan Show* was the only place you could see it. Even though their music was everywhere, we had never seen them live. It was a shared joyous moment for an entire generation and still is today.

"For example, the February 16 performance was from Miami's Deauville Hotel, not from a studio. The quality of the tape image was very fragile. We went back and improved it frame by frame."

With a running time of more than 250 minutes, *The 4 Complete Ed Sullivan Shows Starring the Beatles* have these shows uncut, including not only all of the other performances but also all of the original commercials. The audio is available in both mono and a 5.1 remix. Also housed on the two-DVD set is material from other *Sullivan shows*, notably a short interview with the Beatles that had not been seen since its original television airing in 1964.

Few moments of the Beatles' performances had ever been seen before a similar DVD package debuted in 2003, but distribution at that time was via a small independent company.

In addition, the new DVD set has been augmented with approximately 13 minutes of additional footage. The added material, rare Beatles-related gems from other *Sullivan* shows, is placed at the end of each disc.

"The Ed Sullivan Show" photo courtesy of (c) SOFA Entertainment, All Rights Reserved. (http://www.edsullivan.com)

Among the delights is a brief London interview with the Beatles by Sullivan that had not been seen since the day it aired (May 24, 1964); a 1966 black-and-white commercial for Beatles dolls introduced by Sullivan in color; and the host reading a 1967 telegram from the Beatles congratulating him on the renaming of the studio to "The Ed Sullivan Theater."

"For so many people who experienced those first shows originally, including myself," contemplates Solt, "we remember where we were. But we never saw them again. Now we can, and in context—the complete shows—with all the raw energy and excitement, the audience going crazy. There's also a new generation, one that has bought the reissues, the *Rock*

Band video game, seen Paul McCartney play on the marquee of the Ed Sullivan Theater that's the home of *The Late Show with David Letterman*, heard the songs on *American Idol*. They know the music so well even if they were born decades later. A word like timeless gets overused, but it definitely applies to *The 4 Complete Ed Sullivan Shows Starring the Beatles*."

Solt's other credits range from the 1979 TV special *Heroes of Rock and Roll* and the 1981 Warner Brothers theatrical feature film *This Is Elvis* to the 1988 feature documentary *Imagine: John Lennon*, the 1995 TV documentary series *The History of Rock 'n' Roll* and the 2006 home video *Elvis: The Ed Sullivan Shows*. SOFA Entertainment has produced approximately 400 programs for television and home video.

"Sullivan knew how to give a show that was for every generation that might be watching. It was for the kids to the grandparents. And he knew how to bottle lightning. And he also knew, because he had great instincts, not only how to

"The Ed Sullivan Show" photo courtesy of (c) SOFA Entertainment, All Rights Reserved. (http://www.edsullivan.com)

produce a show but who to put on and what order. And he really was the arbiter of taste for a period of time, which was that postwar era, the birth of television, until the birth of the Seventies. It is a remarkable reflection of American history."

In the June 13, 1971, issue of *West*, a magazine supplement in the *Los Angeles Times*, Ed Sullivan capped off his television career to Wayne Warga: "We did it all. And there wasn't really that much more to do. It was nearly impossible to find new acts for the show. Rock groups, our big attraction the last several years, don't do that much television. They make their success and their money in concerts. I'm convinced there is still a place for a show like ours, that there are people who want the kind of thing we offer. We got caught in the squeeze of dropping ratings and network budgets, and so it's over"

Three years after the 1971 cancellation of his TV series, Sullivan died in New York of esophageal cancer.

"The bonus material," adds Solt, "includes some material that is very unusual that we have used and has never been seen since it was out before, which was, Ed flew to England in 1964 and does a two-minute interview with the four Beatles in London just before the release of *A Hard Day's Night*. It's unusual and special. Also these moments where Ed reflects on the Beatles, either coming on or having been on his show, the reaction, the success. But what is really interesting is their great performances and how excited they are. How they are so together."

Solt further commented about the world of black-and-white film that captured the seminal televised musical performances of the Beatles in America:

"I think because the footage is black-and-white it takes you back even more into an era which to today's generation, nobody understands why anything was ever in black-and-white. I think what really comes across is their excitement, their charisma, their talent, and when you start to think those haircuts were considered revolutionary, weird and longhair, that those Beatles boots that they wore were really different, that they were so unusual. And in retrospect it's humorous, but that is Day 1 of the evolution of rock 'n' roll post-Elvis.

"That era of the Sixties starts February 9, 1964, in America. And it is the first time rock 'n' roll ever comes to us. Because before that, rock 'n' roll was an exported item. It was never imported. And they reinvent it and bring it back and it changes the face of American pop music completely. And that happened there and the city goes mad, the country goes wild, the whole place is affected, and the beauty is watching the faces of these four young guys. And then knowing that they've waited for this moment. They came to America with a No. 1 record. They had it all lined up. And they told that to Brian and it happened.

"And for those of us who remember the music arriving around September 1963, by the time they get to February, it's after the John F. Kennedy assassination and we had been through the doldrums of a very horrific time where everything is questioned. Bomb shelters. I never thought I would see grownups running around, crying like the world had ended. I didn't know what was going on, it was so severe.

"And then 10 weeks later or less, these guys land on our shores, and euphoria reins. And this is the moment. And this can now be enjoyed by people around the world in a way that matters," beamed Solt.

On Sunday, February 9, 2014, at 8pm ET/PT, precisely 50 years to the day, date and time of the Beatles groundbreaking debut on *The Ed Sullivan Show*, CBS-TV broadcast a two-hour primetime entertainment special saluting the Beatles and Ed Sullivan relationship that featured performances of

Beatles songs by many of music's biggest stars in HDTV and 5.1 surround sound.

Filmmaker David Leaf's fascinating and informative 2003 retrospective, *Jack Paar: Smart Television*, includes the Beatles' January 3, 1964 *Jack Paar* appearance I saw, first broadcast on PBS, then later released as a DVD by Shout! Factory. Was this pre-recorded piece their debut U.S. TV appearance? Well, sort of.

As Leaf reports, "There's a clip on the web (audio only) of the *NBC Nightly News (The Huntley-Brinkley Report)* of November 18, 1963. That report has a bit of them playing live, but the point of including that in the story, we're told, is to show how you can't hear them because of the screaming fans, who are described as largely 10-to-16-year-old girls.

"In this lengthy 'back of the book' piece," Leaf continues, "legendary correspondent Edwin Newman, known for his love of language but reflecting his erudite taste in music, spent four minutes reporting, tongue firmly in cheek, on the British phenomenon of Beatlemania. In a nod to their Liverpudlian roots, Newman made puns like 'The quality of Mersey' and "Show us no Mersey.' Needless to say, it wasn't a glowing review, nor in referring to rumors of the group's imminent trip to America did Mr. Newman evince much excitement."

An earlier American TV Beatles moment had come on ABC, when the band's single "She Loves You" received mediocre numbers (73 out of 100) on *American Bandstand's* Rate-a-Record segment. A picture of the Beatles shown on the program reportedly provoked laughter.

As for CBS, when Leaf interviewed the legendary CBS newsman Walter Cronkite for *The U.S. vs. John Lennon*, Cronkite mentioned that *CBS Evening News* had a report on

British Beatlemania ready to run at the end of a Friday news program in November 1963 but events had intervened.

"Events," Leaf notes, "was an understated way of referring to the cataclysmic assassination of President Kennedy. When the *CBS Evening News* report on the Beatles finally aired in December," as Cronkite told Leaf, "before the credits had finished rolling on that night's newscast, Ed Sullivan was on the phone, asking me about the Beatles." A great story…except that the Beatles' manager had apparently already inked a three-appearance deal with Sullivan. Regardless, Leaf adds, "the button on the story is that Cronkite became a hero at home by getting his two daughters precious tickets to the landmark live broadcast."

Of course, at that moment, the historic Sullivan telecast was still in the future. But something was brewing. Leaf recounts, "Even though the Beatles were still primarily a UK phenomenon—all of their pre-1964 stateside singles, on labels like Vee-Jay, Swan and Tollie, had flopped—all three networks (yes, there were only *three* back then), in one way or the other, had covered the Beatles. The Paar clip, however, is still historic, because it was their first prime-time TV appearance by the group." Prime-time? Yes. Leaf explains:

"By 1964, Jack Paar was no longer hosting his late night show. In the fall of '62, *The Jack Paar Program* began its run as a weekly series, Paar having quit the daily grind in mid-1962, turning over the reins of *The Tonight Show* to its new host, Johnny Carson." Leaf reminds us, "Mr. Paar was on Friday nights at 10 p.m. The Beatles segment on Paar's program featured a piece of footage (from 1963) of the Beatles performing 'From Me To You' and She Loves You' on the BBC in England. (As an aside, as an indication of how different that era of network TV was from today, Paar actually promoted the Beatles' upcoming appearance on *The Ed Sullivan Show*.)"

Some fans remember the electricity that particular clip created. But Leaf admits that "at that time, I didn't watch Paar's show. In those days, on Friday nights, I would watch *The Twilight Zone* on CBS, then switch over to ABC for the Friday night fights, followed by *Make That Spare*. And I didn't regularly watch the evening news." So, Leaf insists, "I don't think anybody would suggest it was the Beatles on Huntley-Brinkley on NBC, or Cronkite on CBS, or Jack Paar who made the Beatles stars." More to the point, Leaf emphasizes, "I don't think it was *The Ed Sullivan Show* that made the Beatles hitmakers either. After all," as he alludes, "'I Want to Hold Your Hand' (Capitol's first Beatles single, released just after Christmas) was already at No. 1 by the first week of February, the week *before* they were on *Ed Sullivan*. 'She Loves You' had entered the charts the last week of January. Backstage at their Carnegie Hall concert, before their first Sullivan appearance, they were presented with their first gold record.

"So it's clear that prior to the first Sullivan broadcast, the Beatles had broken through to the youth audience. I was already using my allowance to buy Beatles singles. To me and for millions of baby boomers," Leaf fondly recalls, "that broadcast was (big surprise) a landmark in my life and a nationwide coronation, because they delivered. I know exactly where I was sitting at the moment Ed Sullivan introduced them and exactly how I felt. I don't know if I've ever been as jolted with anticipation and excitement by anything since then (with the possible exception of a few historic sports events I attended). What that Sullivan show did was confirm that they were real and perhaps exponentially magnify our aural passion for the Beatles. After 2/9/64, we were hooked." Why?

"Unlike so many wildly anticipated or hyped events that don't live up to expectation," Leaf states, "the Beatles' February 1964 appearances on *The Ed Sullivan Show* (especially that first night) exceeded everything we could have imagined. They could sing and play and were electrifying performers. And, because a lot of us were too young for Elvis and the early rockers, the Beatles were ours—our 'discovery'—something that the older generation and even some older teens didn't necessarily like. Remember all the inane chatter about their hair? We learned to tune it out. We were in love. And for a half-dozen years after that, the Beatles delivered a series of cultural landmarks, generation-defining moments and works of art."

In trying to understand all of this beyond his own experience and wanting to compare his memories and get the perspective of close friends who were much hipper, Leaf points out that "one friend recalls seeing the Jack Paar show and being very excited."

She remembers, "We were waiting for them. And when they arrived, they brought the outside world to us. Until then, we were so American-centric." Contextualizing that moment, she explains, "Even though I was only 11 years old, because I went to an all-girls Catholic school, the nuns, of course, were in love with JFK. So were we. We watched every speech, every press conference. To us, JFK was the biggest rock star. In JFK, we had, for the first time in our young lives, a president who was witty and urbane and educated. And he wasn't embarrassed about it. JFK, having grown up and having been educated (partly) in England (his father was the ambassador to the Court of St. James), he was surrounded by people who were schooled at Cambridge and Oxford. That made him different from almost all other Americans. He was exposed to other ways of life, then truly tested in war.

"I was six when President Kennedy came into my life. Then, all of a sudden, before I was 11, he was gone. And somehow, almost immediately, out of nowhere, there were four people who could fill that empty space. Four people who were witty too. Four people who weren't afraid to make fun of themselves and the press."

Besides the music, why does she think the Beatles connected so deeply? "Unlike JFK, we were thoroughly Americanized. And for a good reason. America had saved the world. Our fathers had fought and won World War II. We didn't even waste any time learning about the rest of the world. We didn't need anything from anybody else. Our world at home was all we needed."

But kids always want something new. "And the Beatles and what they presented and represented was something completely new and unlike anything we'd ever seen. The fact that they had grown up in wartime, had survived it and were bringing their optimism and energy and enthusiasm to us through the music was why I think it is related to the assassination of JFK. They were evidence that you can survive the worst and do great things. They opened up the world to us. It's a long way from Malibu Beach to Carnaby Street. The Beatles took us there in an instant."

Finally, this lifetime fan points out, "While Beatlemania was exciting and just pure fun, eventually, the Beatles taught us great lessons, from 'The Word' to 'All You Need Is Love' to 'Let It Be.'

"Another friend had a different way of describing that moment that I found fascinating. She said, 'the assassination of President Kennedy made for not only a dark winter but a disorienting one. I was already a Beach Boys fan by then, and there was a very vulnerable quality in the music, so it was comforting. But the up-beat feeling of much of the music seemed out of place - even the perfection of the harmonies had that effect on me. The Beatles came along and it was nice to hear people speaking differently. There was even an odd dissonance to the harmonies that seemed to suit the feeling of the time. The Beatles made another perspective real to me, and I needed that at the time'"

Leaf agrees with the musical side of his friend's analysis but isn't so sure about the political part: "It's been said that in the wake of the assassination of President Kennedy, there was a great sadness in the land and the Beatles were the antidote to that, that we needed something new and young and exciting and positive. I guess that was true for some, but I'm not so sure how much of the Beatles' youthful audience was feeling that way. I can only authoritatively speak to my memory of the era, but I don't think 11-year-olds live in the rearview mirror.

"To make sure I wasn't the outlier in this body of thought, I asked another very close friend, a songwriter and musician who loved both JFK and the Beatles, what his memory was. He confirmed my feeling, said that from his point of view, 'their success in the U.S. had almost nothing to do with JFK and everything to do with the transcendent magic of 'I Want to Hold Your Hand.' Of course everyone was terribly sad after the assassination, but once the initial shock began to fade away, life went on pretty much as usual. I was 16 at the time and I didn't know anyone [my age] who was still upset about the assassination by Christmas time 1963.'

"Consciously, that rings true. But subconsciously, we might have been lost. We were certainly hurt. And sure, the Beatles brought energy and optimism that we responded to. But like my older friend, I don't remember thinking in December 1963, 'I sure need something to get me out of this depression.' Quite the contrary—the first time I heard the Beatles, in mid-December 1963, I was baffled. They just sounded strange. Different. The second time I heard them, it was *my* reaction that was different—I was electrified.

"Regardless of why it happened," Leaf says, "the time was obviously right. They weren't just making great records but they were larger than life, unlike so many other groups who, when they performed on TV, seemed to shrink. TV, even small-screen black-and-white images, just seemed to frame and magnify the Beatles' charisma.

"Ultimately, it was their enormous talent that made it work, made it last. Kids are always looking for the next thing, always need something new to scream about. At that moment, whatever alchemy was at work, the Beatles' magic was almost instantaneous. For a while, the screams even drowned out the music. However, when we (by 'we,' I mean the girls) finally shut up and listened, what we all heard was the beginning of what would be a remarkable artistic journey; the Beatles' creative success was, in part, due to the fact that they continued to grow. They never looked down on their audience. They respected us and trusted us to follow them every step of the way as their art evolved."

Leaf, whose Beatles-related work includes the documentary *You Can't Do That: The Making of "A Hard Day's Night"* and the lengthy Beatles chapter for *Capitol Records 1942-1992 Fiftieth Anniversary* book, follows down this professorial road, befitting his current status as an adjunct professor at UCLA's Herb Alpert School of Music: "As to Beatlemania in America, sure, the hype was, at first, generated by Capitol. But hype only works to get your attention. And airplay. Because once we heard the Beatles on the radio, we didn't need anybody to tell us what to think. That's because we knew instantly how the music made us *feel*.

"As pre-teens we didn't analyze it, didn't necessarily know their early sound was derivative. I didn't know back then that they were an amalgamation of the best of American R&B, rock and pop. Clearly, in retrospect, we can hear how they had absorbed it all: Leiber & Stoller, Little Richard, Buddy Holly, the Everly Brothers, the Isley Brothers, the craftsmanship of Brill Building–era writers like Goffin/King and much, much more.

"But especially as I wasn't a musician or versed in musical history, all I knew was that they had created something new, exciting, vibrant. And when we saw them, they looked and acted unlike any other musicians we'd seen before. They were charming, witty and irreverent. Think of the footage from the press conference in New York when they landed. When had baby boomers seen that from something like that, something that was just for them? So, yes, their individual and group personae were part of the magic too.

"Why did it work so well then and why, 50 years later, are they still the most important *everything* to so many of my generation and, arguably, ever? Probably because of one simple truth: they were not just great singers and rockers, but they wrote incredibly great songs, and they wrote them in a seemingly endless stream, album after album, year after year. Rockers. Ballads. Twenty No. 1 hits. Timeless, instant standards like 'Yesterday.' Multi-generational anthems like 'All You Need Is Love.' They were, for seven years, the consistently best and most prolific pop songwriters and record makers of their time, and now, 50 years later, clearly of all time."

As to the historical echo of what happened 50 years ago, Leaf opines, "As impactful as the Beatles' first appearance on Sullivan was, as much as we all remember that moment as the one that changed our lives, it was also their safe introduction to the mainstream, the mass audience, to the moms and dads. Sullivan had the most eyeballs.

"But," Leaf thinks, "in terms of falling forever in love with the Beatles, that may have happened later that year with *A Hard Day's Night*. Seeing the Beatles on the big screen was probably what turned our teenage crush into a lifetime love affair. It was in that movie that they knocked us out with their music and their wit—they had *individual personalities!* And for the vast majority of us who would never see the Beatles in person, it was the one-two punch of the music in the movie and that film (and the next year in color in *Help!*) that made them our best friends.

"As to how it affected the behavior of the biggest bulge in the baby boom, as the late critic Roger Ebert told me during the making of the *A Hard Day's Night* documentary, Ebert could 'feel [his] hair grow as [he] watched' that movie."

Leaf, who teaches a class at UCLA called *Docs That Rock, Docs That Matter*, maintains that "not only is it one of the great music movies of all time, but Richard Lester's directorial work in that movie enormously influenced film and TV. So, finally, it can't escape notice that in a number of the sequences in *A Hard Day's Night* (and *Help!* which Lester also directed) the modern music video is essentially born. Like their first rock 'n' roll hero, Elvis Presley, had done nearly a decade earlier, in 1964 the Beatles were 'the big bang' of rock that changed everything."

Before he was a member of the Monkees as Davy Jones, actor/singer David Jones, who was playing the Artful Dodger in a Broadway production of *Oliver!* at the Imperial Theatre, shared the same Sullivan marquee when the Beatles debuted.

"When I was on *The Ed Sullivan Show*, it was the first time the Beatles appeared in America," Jones told Monkees archivist Gary Strobl. "Georgia Brown, Clive Revill and different people were in *Oliver!* with me.

"It was interesting. During *Oliver!* we had occasion to go on the show. I was standing in the elevator and Ringo Starr got in. He's obviously a nice chap and he's got his qualities, but he was an ugly bugger, you know? He had this massive nose. Pop singers were sort of like Dave Clark and Paul McCartney. I always tell a joke about Ringo. I said I met him in the elevator, he had a bad cold at the time, and he was about to blow his nose and I said, 'No, let me hold the handkerchief— I'm closer than you are.' And Ringo said, 'I know.'

"And then, all these girls started screaming at the Beatles. All these guys were coming right down and jumping on the Beatles and saying, 'You know, I got my first set of drumsticks because of you.' I wanted a piece of that action.

"And then I saw what happened on the show, and I couldn't believe it. And that's when it first struck me. Within two, three weeks, I was signed to Colpix Records and I was in the studio making some demos."

"The Beatles changed everything," declares musician Henry Diltz, then in the Modern Folk Quartet. "They took our Everly Brothers harmony and put it together with that skiffle music and came up with a new joyful thing.

"As folk musicians in early 1964 we heard and saw them on *The Ed Sullivan Show.* The MFQ (Diltz, Jerry Yester, Chip Douglas, Cyrus Faryar), pulled into a motel, rented a room and watched them on television. We saw them and said, 'Wow.' We want to make music like that. Why are we singing about the ox driver? We want to make joyful music, and we need to get an electric bass and trade in our upright bass. So did every other folk group, like the Byrds and then Buffalo Springfield.

"In 1964 our band, the MFQ were in New York. And we were with a big agency and we did get booked for *The Ed Sullivan Show*. We cancelled our appearance. It was Cyrus and Rusty's (Renais's) Ouija board that said New York was going to sink into the sea. That's exactly how it was put, 'Sink into the sea.' The others weren't all that crazy about the idea either. It made our manager Herbie Cohen absolutely nuts."

Modern Folk Quartet, 1964, photo courtesy of Henry Diltz

"After we rented a motel to watch *The Ed Sullivan Show*, from that moment on we didn't get haircuts," divulged Jerry Yester.

"When the Beatles were on *The Ed Sullivan Show* that was the magical moment for everybody on the East Coast who was doing folk music. Chip Douglas picked up an electric bass shortly after that. I got an acoustic electric guitar. It was like a tadpole that kept growing legs. We hired a drummer for one gig that we did at the Night Owl right before we moved, and just started changing into a rock group. It was obvious that's where all the energy was. That's what we wanted to do.

"The Beatles were like the spokesmen for everybody our age and everybody in our business," said Yester. "Folk music was just dying out as a way of expressing yourself musically. Everybody knew it, but nobody knew what they wanted to do with it. It was like, *Bam!* It was the catalyst, it unified everybody. I swear, a month later there were no more folk clubs in the Village—they were all little rock clubs. The same people were playing there but they were starting to do rock music. The Lovin' Spoonful sprung up. In the space of about six months, people started recording. John Sebastian was doing some rock recordings. So was producer Erik Jacobsen. Everybody worked with everybody else, playing and singing, and it was really exciting."

In October 2013 at a Hollywood media launch celebrating Ringo Starr's *Photograph* book from Genesis Publications, Dave Grohl, the Foo Fighters founder and guitarist/songwriter, talked about watching the Beatles on [a video of] *Ed Sullivan*. "It's a cool thing when you're a human being and you turn on a television and then you see other human beings doing something that moves you so much that you want to do that too.

"I've interviewed people and asked them about their first musical memory, and I swear, nine out of 10 of them cite that as their biggest influence as a musician. Because, you know, in a way I think sometimes the music, or rock 'n' roll, or rock stars, you see it as sort of this two-dimensional thing that doesn't seem real or tangible or people. But then if you see four human beings doing this thing and you think, 'Wow. I'm a person too. Maybe I can do that as well.' That's huge. That's powerful. So, I mean, that's it. You see something that cool and look that cool singing something that sounds that cool but could be that cool."

Two of America's foremost nonfiction filmmakers, Albert Maysles and his brother David (1932–1987), are recognized as pioneers of "direct cinema," the distinctly American version of French cinéma vérité. It is a method in documentary in which events are recorded that couple naturalistic techniques without pre-planned setups or agendas.

They earned their distinguished reputations by being the first to make nonfiction feature films: films in which the drama of human life unfolds as is, without scripts, sets, or narration.

The Maysles were also the first to capture the Beatles' first U.S. visit, chronicling the remarkable two weeks in February 1964 that began America's still-enduring love affair with the group in their *Here's What's Happening Baby— The Beatles!* The celluloid document caught the hysterical reaction to the Beatles that was the real-life inspiration for *A Hard Day's Night.*

David and Albert were granted all-area access to the lads, shadowing them in dressing rooms, hotels, press conferences, and outdoor photo sessions, as they traveled from New York to Washington, D.C., and Miami. Manic moments were woven around frenzied fans from the Beatles' arrival to America on Pan Am Flight 101 to New York. In the process it established the benchmark for rock 'n' roll cinematography. The Maysles' 1964 footage is now incorporated into a more recent retail DVD, *The Beatles: The First U.S. Visit*.

Born in Boston to Jewish immigrants from Eastern Europe, Albert received his B.A. at Syracuse and his M.A. at Boston University, where he taught psychology for three years.

He made the transition from psychology to film in the summer of 1955 by taking a 16mm camera to Russia to film patients at several mental hospitals. The result, *Psychiatry in Russia*, was Albert's first foray into filmmaking.

In 1960, Albert was co-filmmaker of *Primary*, a film about the Democratic primary election campaigns of Kennedy and Hubert H. Humphrey. The use of handheld cameras and synchronous sound allowed the story to tell itself.

Later came his and his brother's landmark nonfiction feature film *Salesman* (1968), a portrait of four door-to-door Bible salesmen from Boston. It won an award from the National Society of Film Critics and is regarded as a classic American documentary. In 1992, the Library of Congress saluted the film for its historical, cultural and aesthetic significance.

Albert was made a Guggenheim Fellow in 1965. His next three films became cult classics. After *Salesman* was *Gimme Shelter* (1970), the dazzling portrait of the Rolling Stones on their 1969 North American tour that culminated in a killing at the notorious concert at Altamont.

During 1994, Albert reunited with the band to film an up-to-date portrait, *Conversations with the Rolling Stones,* which was broadcast on VH1. Recently he revisited them once again with the film *Get Yer Ya-Ya's Out!* (2009), a chronicle of the Stones' epic performance at Madison Square Garden in November 1969.

In 2011, Albert released *The Love We Make*, which followed Paul McCartney through the streets of New York City in the immediate aftermath of the 9/11 attacks as he organized an all-star benefit concert, The Concert for New York City, in the fall of 2001. The 16mm film, shot in black-and-white and co-directed by Maysles and his filmmaking partner Bradley Kaplan, made its debut on the Showtime cable network.

Albert Maysles and Harvey Kubernik Interview

Q: Your *Here's What's Happening Baby—The Beatles!* 1964 documentary movie captured the inside story of the band's first two frenzied weeks in America during February '64. It chronicled the hysterical reaction to the Beatles' U.S. debut, glimpsed on television by their *The Ed Sullivan Show* booking. You and your brother were granted all-area access. Hotel rooms, a trek to a discotheque together. It obviously serves as the real-life inspiration for the movie *A Hard Day's Night*. This century your original documentary was integrated into a new retail DVD from Apple/Capitol, *The Beatles: The First U.S. Visit*. How did this happen?

A: On February 7, 1964, I got a telephone call from Granada Television, whom I never had worked with, but I think they had seen my first film, *Showman*, about Joseph E. Levine. And they said, "The Beatles are arriving in two hours at JFK Airport. Would you like to film them?" So I put my hand over the phone and immediately turned to my brother David and asked him: "Who are the Beatles? Are they any good?" Fortunately, David knew. "Oh. They're great." And he had a big smile on his face.

We both got on the phone and made a deal for TV and rushed out to the airport just in time to see the plane coming in to land. David had his sound recorder and I had my camera. We jumped in the limo with them and off we were running, so to speak. We drove with them into New York City and spent the next four or five days with them.

When the Beatles actually went to *The Ed Sullivan Show* I didn't go inside and watch the performances. Better than that, when they walked into CBS to do *Sullivan*, we realized there was no point in going with them. Because to film them, we would have to go through the whole union process. And by the time we started on that, they would be out of there. So instead, we just walked down the street, got into an ordinary tenement building, we're on the third floor, heard music from a household, knocked on the door, and filmed a family watching the *Sullivan* show. So that was much better.

It's always trying to get behind the scenes to get close towards what is going on. We did go to the Beatles' Washington, D.C., show. There were two versions of the film. That wasn't the Beatles. That was their management—"Make it more commercial." That was broadcast in 1964 on CBS-TV as *The Beatles in America.*

Q: What was going through your mind during your time with the Beatles? Did you have any clue you'd be talking about them 50 years later?

A: *[Laughs.]* I was as mystified as the public was. People have said when they arrived at the airport maybe 10 or 20 people would show up. But instead, 5,000 when they got off the plane.

Q: You and David captured so many aspects of their initial U.S. landing. Footage of their manager Brian Epstein in action, the very popular New York DJ Murray the K conducting and broadcasting a live hotel-room interview with the lads, and then over to the discotheque. Plus, you got things like fans at the hotel corridor and the fascination of the Beatles by the print and photographers.

A: Yes. We had access, but we had confidence that no matter what, no matter whom, if I should film I'll get the OK and film it. But we weren't aware at the time we were a witness to history.

**Beatles In America ad
courtesy Gary Pig Gold Archives**

Author, record producer, music publisher and talent manager (miraculously guiding the Rolling Stones from 1963 to 1967) Andrew Loog Oldham, a current DJ on Little Steven's Underground Garage channel on the Sirius XM satellite radio network, weighs in on the Beatles coming to American towns.

"The British fashion business was the first pop business," instructs Andrew. "Look at the photographic work of Terence Donovan and Bailey in 1960, 1961 in Vogue and you'll see the first Beatles and Stones covers and the clues at all early video attempts. Vidal Sassoon exported his haircuts, Mary Quant exported the miniskirt, David Bailey was already traveling the world for *Vogue*. At the same time poor British pop music had its moments, grand magical moments like Jack Good's TV shows *Oh, Boy!* and *Boy Meets Girl,* but the music we had was hardly exportable. All that ever got out and onto the *Ed Sullivan* TV show and the American airwaves was the one-offs and the freaks—Acker Bilk, Jackie Dennis and Laurie London."

At 16 Andrew landed his first job working as a gofer for the fashion designer Mary Quant. At the same time he worked nights hanging hats and coats at the famous Ronnie Scott's Jazz Club, then located in Soho on Gerrard Street. "I had the best of both worlds," delights Andrew.

"The fashion business was the first British pop business, and I studied with the masters—Mary Quant and her husband Alexander Plunkett Greene. I poured drinks for the journalists and walked the models' dogs and learned where the carpets were thick and the teacups were thin. At night I got my heartbeat attended to working for Ronnie Scott's. I saw Ahmad Jamal, Thelonious Monk, Harold McNair and the great Brits like Ronnie, Tubby Hayes and Stan Tracey.

Oldham would make one last stab at adhering to his mother's wishes with two more jobs in the fashion business, but neither was as challenging as life had been with Mary Quant, and he got bored. He landed on his first set of pop feet when, in 1962, he gained entry into the PR business working for Mark Wynter, a young U.K. popster who gained his success via successful covers of the U.S. hits "Venus in Blue Jeans" and "Go Away Little Girl." In short order Andrew cut his pop teeth repping the tours of Sam Cooke, Little Richard and Jet Harris, along with Johnny "Running Bear" Preston (for promoter Don Arden) and Chris Montez and Tommy Roe (for Arthur Howes).

"My muse, a great lady named Jean Lincoln. I later met Phil Walden through her. She is one of the people who opened the door for me when I was 17 and trying to make a go of it as a PR. She managed the singer Kenny Lynch, who had a U.K. hit with 'Up on the Roof' in '62. She gave me Kenny's PR account and we had some great times together."

In February of the same 1963 Oldham made another main inroad into his future. Attending the pop TV show *Thank Your Lucky Stars* with Wynter, Oldham got "taken over" by a group from Liverpool rehearsing their spot in the show.

"Groups from Liverpool were not in the daily run of things in the front of '63," underscores Oldham. "Groups usually had their hair greased back, not dry and forward. I was watching the Beatles do 'Please Please Me' and I was taken by their sound, the song, their sense of image and the possibility of another client. They were laconic as opposed to desperate. I spoke to the Beatle who seemed the most approachable to me—John Lennon. I asked him who handled him, and he pointed me in the direction of Brian Epstein."

Between January and April of 1963 Andrew represented the Beatles and Brian Epstein's other new acts, Gerry & the Pacemakers and Billy J. Kramer and the Dakotas, and spent one of the most productive and carefree times of his life. He made sure the Beatles were interviewed by Penny Valentine and placed the group into *Beat Instrumental*, too.

"I was doing the Beatles' PR in early '63 and Kenny Lynch and the Beatles were on a tour with Tommy Roe and Helen Shapiro. It was over that tour, between 'Please Please Me' and 'From Me To You,' that you saw the chaos and the pandemonium grow to explosive proportions. Something had to give—the U.K. was bursting at its Beatled seams—and what finally gave was America.

"I was representing this fascinating wonder, the Beatles. I liked Brian Epstein and the way he got things done. The English managers were promoting music the establishment hoped would go away and the American managers were promoting American music, an art that they were not ashamed of."

Epstein and Oldham in 2014 were both inducted into the Rock and Roll Hall of Fame, a non-performing honor, and received Ahmet Ertegun awards.

I once asked Andrew in an interview that ran in *DisCoveries* magazine what he learned from Epstein.

"What did I learn from Brian? Oh, the danger of being in love with the act—a lesson I'm glad to say I didn't learn. That paisley scarf didn't suit me. That if you've been lucky enough to have had an education, use the accent—it works. Brian was a lovely, passionate but tortured man.

"The recent revisionist shit about 'Our Brian' with his life and too many queens' wishful thinking served up as British TV fodder is vomit-laden and appalling. John Lennon had a much blunter take on it all.

"Let us look at the bottom line. Brian was a passionate man who would not take a 'no' on behalf of his lads, and that is how we got to hear the Beatles music. Anyway, as I've said before, we all owe Brian a huge debt for getting the Beatles their recording contract. I mean, we would not be chatting now had the only U.K. hits in America been the Tornados, Petula Clark and Acker Bilk. End of story. The rest is all schadenfreude, anal-retentive scatology and self-serving revisionism.

"For one, it was obvious that 'this thing of ours' was not going to disappear. We had come in following the twist, Davy Crockett, skiffle, and trad jazz. Skiffle and trad jazz had been very important; they had been the BBC and the Establishment's last chance to control the key to what music we got to hear. You had shows like *The 6.5 Special*, hosted by Pete Murray—God bless him!—and Jo Douglas, which invited us all to deck up in jeans and sweaters and be really daring with our shirt collars turned up.

"The music was shite, with a few exceptions, like Lonnie Donegan, whose earnestness and belief was almost evangelical. The rest were a bunch of lame skiffers and jazz musicians who thought they were in a lamentable kindergarten, which they were. Yes, we had Eddie Cochran, Little Richard, Duane Eddy and Buddy Holly and the rest, but it had been a fight.

"You see, before the Beatles went to America, the best possibility that pop music offered was not having to get a regular job. You must remember that Ringo would have happily called it a hard day's night if he'd made enough money to open a ladies' hair salon and settle down with Maureen. Life was that simple until America entered the equation. It was an age of innocence that ended when America became a possibility. America seized the Beatles in the same way people seized Davy Crockett and Hula-Hoops.

"Then the Beatles played *The Ed Sullivan Show.* That moment when American youth, feeling the subtext, feeling the great unspoken hurt of a nation still traumatized by the assassination of its president just a few months before. It's an incredible moment: suddenly American youth had its own music, a reason to be alive."

On January 3, 1964 Vee-Jay released "Please Please Me" (with B-side "From Me To You"), and the Beatles' first Capitol album, *Meet The Beatles!*, followed on January 20. After achieving the No. 1 chart position for five consecutive weeks in the U.K., "I Want to Hold Your Hand" reached the top of the U.S. singles chart on February 1, holding the No. 1 position for seven consecutive weeks, and within two months, more than 3.5 million copies of *Meet The Beatles!* were sold in the U.S.

Just before the Beatles met the Maysles brothers and their first slot on *The Ed Sullivan Show* on February 9, I heard a commercial on KFWB, my AM radio station in L.A., about the Beatles, Beach Boys and Lesley Gore's appearance together in March from Washington, D.C., Coliseum that we could see at the local Fox Wilshire Theater! The place was literally around the corner from our house in Los Angeles.

When the Beatles were on *Ed Sullivan* it was an event! They became a verb that night; I remember feeling like a bolt of lightning jolted our Wilshire District–area family home. These tiny people on screen were now engraved on the country's brain.

I quickly realized there were more records outside in another world than B.B. King, the Beach Boys, Jan & Dean, Little Richard, Elvis Presley, Del Shannon, Chris Montez,

Sam Cooke, the Miracles, the Ventures, Frank Sinatra, Julie London, Timi Yuro, Hayley Mills and the Ronettes to hear.

These guys were from England. But their records didn't sound anything like clarinet player Acker Bilk's "Stranger on the Shore" or "Midnight in Moscow" from Kenny Ball and His Jazzmen, two earlier 45 RPM singles that radio station KRLA (1110 AM) would often spin.

I bought their first two 45s at Wallichs Music City in Hollywood. Then the Capitol long player at the Wilshire Boulevard May Company department store. I purchased the Vee-Jay long player at Norty's record shop on Fairfax Ave. In 1964 I got all my vinyl Beatles at the Frigate at 3rd Street and Crescent Heights Ave. And later in '64 my first ever U.K. Beatles and Rolling Stones British import LPs from Lewin Record Paradise on Hollywood Boulevard.

After captivating North America with their *Ed Sullivan* debut, The Beatles traveled to Washington, DC, performing their first Stateside concert on February 11 at the Washington Coliseum to 8,000 fans in the round.

When the Beatles first came to the U.S. in 1964, primarily to appear on *The Ed Sullivan Show*, they also arranged two live concerts. The first of these concerts—their first ever in

> MAKE THE
> **LEWIN**
> **Record Paradise**
> 6507 Hollywood Blvd.
> (at N. Wilcox)
> HO 4-8088
>
> **Your Headquarters**
> **For All Your Favorite**
> **45's and L.P.s**
>
> ALL ENGLISH GROUPS
> ALWAYS IN STOCK
>
> *Our Prices Will Please You*
> *Everything Here Real "Neat"*
>
> Come in and see new and unusual photos of Beatles and Stones

Lewin Record Paradise ad courtesy of Jim Roup

the U.S.—occurred in Washington, D.C., at the Washington Coliseum on February 11.

The Beatles also made another live stop during their February 1964 U.S. visit—at New York City's Carnegie Hall on February 12. In New York there were two shows, but in Washington, only one. It was filmed in black-and-white video by CBS with the permission of the Beatles' manager, Brian Epstein.

This historic outing was videotaped for a national closed-circuit theater viewing audience, and then packaged a month later with pre-taped television studio live sets by the Beach Boys and Lesley Gore for a 90-minute silver screen event, *The Beatles: Direct From Their First American Concert*, that was broadcast in over 100 North American movie houses, employing a system generally utilized for boxing matches and live sporting broadcasts. The Lesley Gore and Beach Boys segments were videotaped in late January '64 in Burbank, California, at the NBC Television Studios and part of a separate in-studio lensing hosted by local DJ Roger Christian.

The master videotapes of this concert were a leap forward over the third-generation inferior copy kinescopes that have been screened on the midnight movie circuit for nearly half a century. These circulated prints always had the Beatles' encore of the Bert Russell Berns/Phil Medley–crafted "Twist and Shout" cut near the middle of the song. Bootleg copies of the fabled D.C. show also usually didn't contain a rendition of the final number, Little Richard's "Long Tall Sally." Snippets of the March 1964 closed-circuit booking have been utilized for the Beatles *Anthology* and other video collections.

The promoters, National General Corporation and venture partners did extremely well, garnering millions of dollars in the limited rollout of the Beatles/Beach Boys/Gore product.

The Passport Company in 2003 issued a commercial DVD, *The Beatles in Washington D.C., February 11, 1964.*

In 2011, photographs from Mike Mitchell of the Beatles' February news conference and first live concert were unveiled at a Christie's auction in New York City. Mitchell's portraits of the Beatles on that pop-culture-defining moment were the centerpiece of a month-long August 2013 exhibition at the David Anthony Fine Art Gallery in Taos, New Mexico.

Mitchell told Susan Montoya Bryan from the Associated Press in August 2013, "The Beatles were on fire that night." Norman Markowitz, a history professor at Rutgers University in New Jersey, mentioned to her in that AP news report, "The Beatles came to represent some of the yearnings for peace and hope and equality and a larger social justice. In the United States and throughout the world, their personalities became as important as the music."

The Beatles' public appearance at the Washington Coliseum, located at 3rd and M Streets N.E., occurred during a cold and snowy night. It was their first live American performance after their televised appearance on *The Ed Sullivan Show*. It was the longest-ever set filmed of them in concert.

Opening that show were the Caravelles, a British girl duo best known for their 1963 hit record, "You Don't Have to Be a Baby to Cry," Tommy Roe of "Sheila" fame, and the Chiffons, known for "He's So Fine" and "One Fine Day."

When the Beatles came on, the place erupted with screaming and incessant flash bulbs. They played for nearly an hour. Because of the setup in the Coliseum, the Beatles were essentially performing on a boxing-ring-type stage, requiring them to move their equipment around onstage a few times in order to give everyone in the audience a chance to see them.

Ringo was seen moving his drum set around on stage between songs, aided by road manager Mal Evans.

Beatles Set List -- Washington, D.C. -- February 1964

Roll Over Beethoven

From Me To You

I Saw Her Standing There

This Boy

All My Loving

I Wanna Be Your Man

Please Please Me

Till There Was You

She Loves You

I Want to Hold Your Hand

Twist and Shout

Long Tall Sally

Paul McCartney called it "the most tremendous reception I have ever heard in my life."

In 1975 I asked Mal Evans, then living in Los Angeles, during a Keith Moon recording session at the L.A. Record Plant, about that frenzied recital. Mal smiled and replied, "Oh yes…That was a good one!"

After their live D.C. conquest, the group went to a ball at the city's British Embassy.

Part 1: Nick of Time

Ad for closed circuit Beatles, Beach Boys, Lesley Gore Concert Telecast courtesy of Gary Pig Gold Archives

The Beatles that day returned to New York by train for their Carnegie Hall concerts—two 25-minute performances before 2,900 fans attending each show.

About a month later, in mid-March 1964, *The Beatles: Direct From Their First American Concert*—the complete 90-minute film of the Beatles' D.C. show with footage of

Beach Boys and Lesley Gore performances—was transmitted over telephone lines to selected U.S. and Canadian theaters in four separate shows—two each day—over the weekend of March 14-15, 1964.

Among the receiving theater locations that Saturday were the Stanley Theater in Pittsburgh, Pennsylvania; the Hippodrome Theater in Cleveland, Ohio; the El Monte Legion Stadium in El Monte, California and in Los Angeles at the Stanley Warner Wiltern Theatre.

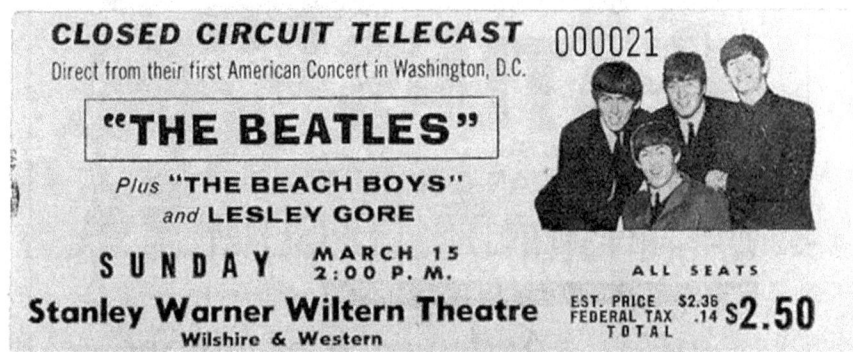

The Beatles, Beach Boys and Lesley Gore Concert ticket image courtesy of Gary Pig Gold Archives

The total audience for the Beatles' concert film was expected to exceed 500,000. The shows were seen in more than 100 theaters in the U.S. and Canada. The promoters—identified in advertising as the National General Corporation, or their subsidiary, Theater Color Vision—made millions.

One 1964 estimate placed the take at some $4 million, or roughly $30 million in today's money. This Beatles-driven package was possibly the first use of closed-circuit broadcasting for a rock concert, as previously this theater network had been used only for championship boxing matches.

I went to the Fox Wilshire Theater. Afterwards I truly thought (and really felt) the Beatles, the Beach Boys and Lesley Gore were in the room with us!

It was obvious my response had nothing to do with previously having witnessed in person Superman (George Reeves), Gene McDaniels, Judy Garland, Barbra Streisand, the Beach Boys, Dick Dale, Eddie Cano, Earl Grant, Freddie Blassie, Frank Sinatra, Steve Allen, Keely Smith and Louis Prima, Soupy Sales, and Spike Jones with Helen Grayco.

I now felt the world had changed right in front of me. But it was now thrilling, exciting, and safe, and not something gripping and scaring me from a 1959–1963 first-run *Twilight Zone* episode.

And one of the Beatles was left-handed like guitar player and surfer Dick Dale! The Dodgers' baseball pitcher Sandy Koufax was also a southpaw.

There was a telling aftermath from this *Tall Boy* five-ton-like musical bomb dropping that had just struck the fringes of Beverly Hills. The Fox Wilshire was the same room that in 1963 ran one of my favorite movies, the aptly futuristic *The Great Escape*. Every schoolgirl around me wet and soaked their cushioned seats scant minutes after the curtain opened. Hysterical screams of release.

Quincy Jones was Lesley Gore's record producer in 1964, and Gore's inclusion in this Beatles blockbuster perhaps acknowledged the role Jones once tried to play in garnering the Beatles a cherished U.S. label deal.

After Jones returned from Europe in 1961, Irving Green at Mercury Records hired him as an A&R man. Green promoted him to vice president the following year, making Jones the first African American with such a position at a white-owned label. In his new role, he worked doggedly as a producer, arranger, and touring musical director for several artists.

Quincy discovered Lesley Gore during this time and began producing her teen hits. In addition, from 1961 to 1965 Jones made records for Dizzy Gillespie, Dinah Washington, Brook Benton, Peggy Lee, Sarah Vaughan, Count Basie, Ella Fitzgerald, Frank Sinatra, Sammy Davis Jr., and Billy Eckstine.

It was Quincy who heard the Beatles literally before anyone in America, around his jazz, pop and R&B sessions. Brian Epstein touted the group. Little Richard, fresh off some European gigs with the Beatles, was newly signed to Vee-Jay in the USA. Jones produced Little Richard's return to rock, *The King of Gospel Singers*, in 1962.

After a *Billboard* magazine 1977 Disco Convention panel at Century Plaza Hotel in Los Angeles, Quincy and I talked briefly about how he attempted to secure an American record deal for Epstein's label-less boys in 1962 and early 1963.

Quincy told me he saw the Rolling Stones and the Beatles before they came to the United States and that they were fantastic. Jones even bet with Lennon and McCartney against George Harrison and Ringo Starr and Brian Epstein that the Beatles would not make the charts in America. Didn't think at the time that a U.K. act could break the dominance of American music.

"The only time I've ever heard the Fabs and the Q used in the same sentence was Lennon and McCartney asking George Martin in '63 how to get 'the Lesley Gore sound' on their vocals—hence the double-tracking from the *With the Beatles* sessions onwards," confirms Toronto Beatlemaniac-for-life Gary Pig Gold.

"Lesley was blessed with a most expansive and expressive voice to begin with, of course. In a recent New York club appearance of hers I was fortunate to attend, she remarked how Quincy nicknamed her 'Little Bits,' marveling at such big sounds coming from such a small girl. But under his perfect guidance, those early records of hers somehow almost scaled Phil Spector's sonic Wall!

"Meanwhile, from the opposite coast, the Beach Boys positively wail through footage from that prehistoric period before even *The T.A.M.I. Show*. Look closely too, and you can even spot promoter Fred Vail and the future Mrs. Brian Wilson in the audience as Mike Love removes his shoes and picks up his sax. The Beach Boys' set is culled from their first five LPs, where Brian Wilson, Carl Wilson, Dennis Wilson, Al Jardine and Mike Love are a cohesive team.

"So, packaging the Wilsons, Lesley, and those grand new Beatles all into one evening's mega-entertainment was one rare case of a money-grab which actually made history: Three decades after its initial screenings, the Beatles' set was still being spliced and diced into various Apple-sanctioned home-video releases, while the Beach Boys' footage was wisely issued intact as *The Lost Concert*. Both constitute nothing short of Required Viewing for anyone who consider themselves true rock 'n' rollers…or even Canadians."

The hesitancy of America to invest in the Beatles extended to several U.S. record companies winding from Chicago to L.A. "I was asked in 1963 to listen to this group the Beatles," volunteered songwriter P.F. Sloan, who in '63 worked as a staff writer for a Hollywood-based publishing company.

"If anyone came from England at the time, they were dead in the water. The only people were Lonnie Donegan, Frank Ifield, Cliff Richard. I listened to this demo of 'Love Me Do' and 'Thank You Girl' and was asked what I'd thought of it. I said, 'Don't ask me why, but this is the best thing I've ever heard.' And they said, 'We know that you're pretty crazy, so we're going to pass on this,'" Sloan told DJ Roger Steffens in a 1987 radio interview.

"They took a chance anyway, and the people put it out on Vee-Jay. And Vee-Jay was going broke, and this was their last record that they were ever going to put out and it happened to be the Beatles. And it took a while before everything happened.

"I played guitar and harmonica on [Barry McGuire's] 'Eve of Destruction' and wrote it. I was on a tour in London of my own, 'Eve of Destruction' was No. 1, and the Grass Roots' 'Where Were You When I Needed You,' [which] I wrote, was in the Top 10. I went to one of the clubs. McCartney was there, and [he] asked me, 'What's this load of rubbish about the 'Eve of Destruction'? I talked to John Lennon, and Lennon thinks this is a load of rubbish. Won't have none of it.'"

Boy From the Real North Country

"Growing up in Canada during the mid-Sixties as a 10-year-old constantly craving rock 'n' roll did have its distinct advantages," admits Gary Pig Gold. "For example, I remember 'yeah-yeah-yeah'-ing along to 'She Loves You' back when Dale & Grace were still busy topping the American charts.

"The British never needed to invade Canada," explains Gold. "They were *invited.*

"The first ever broadcast of a Beatles recording anywhere in North America was 'Love Me Do' on CFRB Toronto's weekly *Calling All Britons* show, December 1962.

"Also, 'Please Please Me' charted during April of '63 on CFGP-AM, Grande Prairie, Alberta, three months before 'From Me To You' charted on KRLA, which is usually cited as the Beatles' first chart placing in North America.

Part 1: Nick of Time

SILVER DOLLAR SURVEY

GRANDE PRAIRIE'S OFFICIAL RECORD SURVEY

THIS WEEK	WEEK ENDING APRIL 27, 1963		LAST WEEK
1	Mecca	Gene Pitney (United Artists)	1
2	I Will Follow Him	Peggy March (RCA)	3
3	Peanuts	The 4 Seasons (Reo)	7
4	In Dreams	Roy Orbison (Monument)	4
5	Pipeline	The Chantays (Dot)	2
6	Sandy	Dion (Laurie)	16
7	Summer Holiday	Cliff Richard (Capitol)	9
8	Over The Mountain	Bobby Vinton (Epic)	18
9	Puff	Peter, Paul and Mary (Warner Bros.)	8
10	Surfin' U.S.A.	The Beach Boys (Capitol)	6
11	Gypsy Heart	Bobby Curtola (Tartan)	11
12	He's So Fine	The Chiffons (Laurie)	5
13	My First Love	Babs Tino (Kapp)	13
14	Little Band of Gold	James Gilreath (Joy)	14
15	Daddy Couldn't Get Me One of Those, Helen Shapiro (Cap.)		15
16	Dancing Shoes	Cliff Richard (Capitol)	17
17	Initials	The Castells (London)	NEW
18	Killer Joe	The Rockey Fellers (Quality)	26
19	I got Burned	Ral Donner (Reprise)	28
20	Here I Stand	The Rip Chords (Columbia)	30
21	Tom Cat	The Rooftop Singers (Vanguard)	21
22	A Cake and a Candle	Emily Evans (London)	20
23	Move Along Baby	Les Paul and Mary Ford (Columbia)	74
24	Back in Baby's Arms	Patsy Cline (Decca)	25
25	Linda	Jan and Dean (Liberty)	63
26	Count On Me	Tommy Roe (Sparton)	19
27	Please Please Me	The Beatles (Capitol)	34
28	Heart	Kenny Chandler (Laurie)	22
29	Another Saturday Night	Sam Cooke (RCA)	NEW
30	Charms	Bobby Vee (Liberty)	23
31	On Broadway	The Drifters (Atlantic)	43
32	Bo Diddley	Buddy Holly (Coral)	62
33	The Wayward Wind	Vince Howard (London)	79
34	Sympathy	Wanda Jackson (Capitol)	24
35	Don't Wanna Think About Paula ?-?-?? (Mercury)		72
36	One Broken Heart For Sale	Elvis Presley (RCA)	10
37	I Got A Woman	Rick Nelson (Decca)	29
38	Two Kinds of Teardrops	Del Shannon (Quality)	NEW
39	Insult To Injury	Timi Yuro (Liberty)	NEW
40	The Bird's The Word	The Rivingtons (Liberty)	81

CFGP PICK HIT: — PATTY BABY, Fred Cannon (Quality)

LISTEN FOR -- COMPLETE NEWS COVERAGE
featuring
Lionel Kyle - Bob Sharples

CFGP Canada survey sheet courtesy of Gary Pig Gold Archives

"Capitol Records there, much unlike their big brothers down in the States, loved and released Beatles records right from 'Love Me Do' onwards. And while they didn't initially sell as well as, say, Capitol of Canada's Cliff Richard releases, by the time of 'She Loves You,' even mighty 1050 CHUM-AM in Toronto were going all-out for all things mop-top. In fact, the Canadian *Beatlemania!* album—identical in content and even packaging (save for some added front-cover verbiage from the Ottawa Journal) to none other than *With the Beatles*—was the first Beatle long player released *anywhere* in North America.

**CHUM Radio Hit Parade Top Ten Hits of January 27, 1964
courtesy of Gary Pig Gold Archives**

"Of course, Canada has always enjoyed extremely close-knit ties with Britain. *Everyone* has dear friends and family back in the homeland, and in 1963 many of the newspaper clippings and even vinyl they were sending over to the colony concerned that big beat seeping down from

Merseyside. Soon, those young Canucks already blessed with their own drum kits and guitars were busy learning and adding the latest Pacemakers and Billy J. [Kramer] B-sides to their sets, thrilling local audiences with this strange new sound and style which, when it finally hit stateside big time on the 2/9/64 *Ed Sullivan Show*, already seemed somewhat old hat to with-it kids in Winnipeg.

"In fact, as no less an authority on all things Beatles, Canada-style as Burton Cummings offers, 'we heard the English Invasion early. Why do you think I end my solo piano concerts with 'Ferry Cross the Mersey'?

"Meanwhile," Gold continues, "in the fab fervor which engulfed all of America immediately post-Sullivision, it was none other than good ol' Capitol Canada who came to the rescue of Yankee pressing plants already swamped with 'I Want to Hold Your Hand' and *Meet the Beatles!* back orders, by exporting down to key New York retailers tens of thousands of Canadian 'Roll Over Beethoven,' 'All My Loving' and 'Twist and Shout' 45s.

"So then, as the Beatles were not the first *or* last to demonstrate, it always seems best, and easiest, to get irrevocably into America by way of that big back door up North.

"However, when it came to actually seeing my new favorite group, us Torontonians had to patiently await a certain *Ed Sullivan Show* just like the rest of North America.

"But save for several solid faux-concert scenes in *A Hard Day's Night*, it wasn't until the extremely late Seventies, via an embargoed video machine in a local Media Arts college, that I was able to view an entire set of vintage '64 Beatles in action for myself. And that footage, scratchy and blurred and worse for all the countless generations from its original source it may then have been, luckily was of the band's first—and probably still best—American concert ever. Washington, D.C. February 11, 1964.

"Here were four musicians more than happy, hungry, and positively burning with the excitement of finding what seemed to be the entire world at their leather-pointed feet. Making sure to tip hats towards St. Louis' own Chuck Berry with their opening 'Roll Over Beethoven' and not once letting the fervor drop from then onwards, these were Beatles firing on cylinders I'd bet even they didn't think existed. Ringo especially flails and pounds with a flash and determination which would reach forward at least to Nirvana's Dave Grohl, while his accomplices that evening more than rise above faulty microphones, flying jelly beans, and a drum riser which appeared to be left over from a Three Stooges recital. If there was better music being made anywhere in the world on this particular night, I for one have yet to hear, or even hear about it."

This was, of course, just after Capitol USA had finally issued their American-edition debut "I Want to Hold Your Hand" single and *Meet the Beatles!* album, having spent the majority of 1963 turning down all Beatle masters EMI London sent their way. Instead, EMI had simply ordered their American licensing agency, Transglobal, to place the band with any other U.S. label they could find.

Vee-Jay, at that point having great pop success with the Four Seasons, released both "Please Please Me" and its follow-up "From Me To You." Neither was successful, and Vee-Jay was by mid-'63 having severe cash-flow problems. So they passed on both "She Loves You" backed with "I'll Get You" (which Transglobal then leased with Dick Clark's co-owned Philadelphia-based Swan label) and the proposed summer 1963 release of the *Introducing the Beatles* LP.

Part 1: Nick of Time

DICK CLARK MEETS THE BEATLES

In 1999 I visited the sorely missed radio DJ/entrepreneur and entertainment business titan Dick Clark in his Burbank, California office.

The impressive complex was filled with photos of the Beatles, John Lennon, and Stuart Sutcliffe artwork. I quizzed him about the Beatles. Clark showed me a Swan Records staff photo and a record presentation to the Beatles on their first American tour in 1964. "You asked for it," America's oldest teenager warned me. "Here's a ticket stub from November 1961 from a Beatles show which amounts to 42 cents U.S. money.

"Here's the photo of Bernie [Binnick] and Tony [Mammarella], my former partners in Swan, with the Beatles when I was in the music business. After the government forced me out of the music business, they went on with it.

"The first record Bernie brought back was from these four kids from England with the funny haircuts. Another TV mention of the Beatles came when 'She Loves You' received mediocre numbers on *American Bandstand's* Rate-a-Record segment. And the kids gave it a 73. They didn't like it. I thought they looked strange. I didn't particularly care for it, because I thought it was derivative. It sounded like the Crickets and Buddy Holly, and a little Chuck Berry. Recycled old American music. I didn't focus in on the fact that it had a different thrust. I had no idea they would go on and make their own music and change the world.

"The irony of the picture of Bernie and Tony with the Beatles and the record 'She Loves You' was that, had Swan sold 50,000 copies of 'She Loves You' that we played on Rate-a-Record, we would have had the rights to the Beatles ad infinitum.

47

"I said to Bernie years later, 'Why didn't you buy 50,000 copies?' *[Laughs.]* This was their second release. Vee-Jay and Ewart Abner had them first. Bernie was an alert guy. Someone called his attention and he went over to England to check the Beatles out. At the time, Capitol didn't want them in the U.S.

"How fate changes things. We did *Birth of the Beatles*, and Pete Best got aced out of a drummer's job and I met him and talked to him. I wondered, how did this man walk around without being a total nutcase, knowing that he got aced out of a job as one of four musicians who changed the world? He was the technical advisor on our show. A sweet man. I still hear from him."

Dick had caught the Beatles in action on their 1964 U.S. tour.

"I saw them in Atlantic City on their first tour here. The first time I saw them in the flesh. Several times thereafter. It was interesting because it was like the first time I saw Elvis Presley. There was this shriek, this sound, which I think is part of the reason they gave up performing in person. It was very hard to hear the music. The audience reaction was phenomenally interesting. That's what I found about Presley.

"I saw Presley in the '50s at the Arena in Philadelphia, a 4,000-seater. It was the first time my ears rang after a concert. The same thing happened in Atlantic City when I saw the Beatles. So you knew something was going on. We later promoted them in Pittsburgh, I think. We had to pay them $25,000 for the night, which was just incredibly expensive in those days."

"I was in a touring version of the Royal Teens and did things like Dick Clark tours," waxed Al Kooper, strictly a guitar player at the time.

"In late 1957, I watched Buddy Holly & the Crickets from the wings of the Brooklyn Paramount say, 'Here's our brand new single, just out today,' and start playing 'Oh Boy.' I saw from the wings Jerry Lee Lewis set the piano on fire.

"I was living in New York (in 1963) and I was aware of the two other releases by the Beatles before Capitol. At the time I was a full-time songwriter (Keely Smith, Tommy Sands, Freddie Cannon, Bobby Vee, Gene Pitney). I didn't understand it totally until the Capitol record.

"I watched *The Ed Sullivan Show*. It didn't have this big impact on me. The Stones did. I totally got that. I saw the Stones when they played the Academy of Music in New York. It was great."

Dave Hull: The Honorary Fifth Beatle

Another powerful radio personality, Dave "The Hullabalooer" Hull at station KRLA (1110 AM) in Pasadena, California, was blowing his literal horn drawing attention to the Beatles in 1964. It was in some ways a logical extension of the playlist relationship the 50,000-watt station had in the important Southern California AM market.

Courtesy Gary Pig Gold Archives

In my book, *Turn Up the Radio! Rock, Pop and Roll in Los Angeles 1956–1972*, published by Santa Monica Press, Hull discussed the 1964–1970 audio bond KRLA had with the Beatles.

"KRLA and I supported the Rolling Stones and the Beatles. In 1964 and '65, [KRLA DJ] Bob Eubanks presented the Beatles at the Hollywood Bowl, and then at Dodger Stadium in 1966.

"It's important to note that earlier, back in 1961 and '62, KRLA played records from England that were local and national hits. Acker Bilk's 'Stranger on the Shore,' Kenny Ball's 'Midnight in Moscow,' and Hayley Mills' 'Let's Get Together' and 'Cobbler, Cobbler' from the Disney movie *The Parent Trap*.

"I first heard the Beatles' 'Love Me Do' as a promotional record in 1962 on WVKO in Ohio.

"I was close for a bit with Paul McCartney and Brian Epstein, through Derek Taylor. The relationship with them went beyond press conferences and show intros at the Hollywood Bowl and Dodger Stadium.

"I would see the Beatles at the places they rented in town. The closeness I had with the Beatles was owed to Louise Harrison, George's sister, who was the one that gave me inside information, because she wanted her brother George to be part of a famous group. Brian Epstein was the best, but Derek Taylor as his publicity man—he really knew how to advance anyone and go into a market, and press release stuff that would make people want to know the answers to questions before he'd leave town. He was brilliant.

"I came from a world that started with the 45 RPM single. They didn't care about the B-side, just the A-side, and played the poop out of it. Then the LP, the long player, arrived, helped immensely by the Beatles. We are on AM radio. This is before FM rock. One thing about the Beatles, they brought one important thing to the American and worldwide music scene that nobody else did. Before them, like Frank Sinatra, one or two songs, maybe that were gonna be hits, the rest of it filler. When it came to the Beatles, everything they did was great. Therefore you were forced by the Beatles to play the albums, and cuts like 'If I Fell' and 'Girl.' All of these things were not singles first, but taken out by KRLA and played on the air to become such with the market and no one could ever see that coming."

Part 1: Nick of Time

KFWB newspaper ad courtesy of Gary Strobl Archives

Charlene Nowak: It Pays To Listen

Dave Hull on his KRLA radio show gave the home addresses away of all the Beatles in Liverpool. Bonnie, Linda and I picked the home address of George Harrison because we had read in one of the magazines on the Beatles that he answered his fan mail.

At the time I lived in North Hollywood. I was age 16 and was attending Van Nuys High School. We actually did a reel-to-reel tape and sent it to George's mother, talking mostly about our families and schools. The Beatles were in New York when this happened.

We saw the 1964 closed circuit concert with the Beatles, Beach Boys and Lesley Gore in Van Nuys. I was stunned by the reaction of the girls that were sitting in this auditorium screaming at a screen. As far as the concert went I was majorly impressed by their performance. The only thing I ever went to before this was a sock hop at Van Nuys Junior High School where Annette Funicello was the guest.

Three weeks later a letter comes to Bonnie's address from Mrs. Harrison in Liverpool. She had sent us a handwritten letter thanking us for the tape and sent each one of us got a fact sheet on George. An autographed fan club card photo with George's autograph on it. The thing was, we did not have any expectations. And we wrote another letter back to her and thanked her. And she wrote back that she planned to come to the States in August when they were appearing at the Hollywood Bowl and she would like to meet us. We were fans. And then we got a telephone call from Derek Taylor saying that "Mrs. Harrison could not make it to the United States but she still wanted us to meet her son. And we would be compensated."

Of course, after we got off the phone with Derek Taylor there were some hysterics. And then he called back a while later and said it would be August 22nd at the rented house on St. Pierre Road in Bel-Air at 1:00 pm in the afternoon. And could we please refrain from bringing any cameras because the lads have been posing for pictures all week. And this was their time between now and the Hollywood Bowl to relax.

We drove from the San Fernando Valley through Beverly Glen and went past the Bel-Air gates. We went up this hill and reached a barricade between the LAPD and the Bel-Air security. We were on the guest list and we got a lot of taunting from the girls on the other side of the barrier. "Oh you think you're gonna get through..." until they opened up the big black wrought-iron gates and we drove through. We were met at the door by Mal Evans who took us to this enormous Spanish style house with furniture and crystal chandeliers and stuff that none of us had ever seen before.

Derek Taylor met us in the living room. He was dressed in summer clothes. Derek told us the boys were out in the yard. He didn't tell us they were out by the pool in bathing suits. "Let me take you out and introduce you to George." So we went out through these two glass doors that led out to a very small lawn. So we step out and off to the right is the pool. It's fenced in. And there they are. All four in bathing suits. John was sitting at the wet bar with the radio next to him going from KRLA to KFWB to see which one of the stations was playing their song. Ringo was sitting on the diving board dangling his feet in the pool. Paul was in the pool, and George was sitting in a chaise lounge. And then Derek brought us over and introduced us to George. "These are the girls that your mother told us about."

Was I shaking? I could not stand up. We weren't flipping out because we were scared to death. My mouth felt like someone had shoved a wad of cotton in it. George came over and pulled up three chaise lounge chairs and asked us to sit. He went into right away, "So you wrote my Mum." We spent an hour and we talked about his niece and nephew. We talked to how we got his address and we mentioned Dave Hull. Ringo went, "Hello luv." Paul was in the pool swimming laps, "How you doing?" All I could think of was, "Oh my God! They're in bathing suits." Paul got out of the pool with his blue swim trunks that had white stripes going up both sides. And he put on a powder blue terry cloth robe that was a shorty. I kind of knew what boys were. George asked about the weather in the San Fernando Valley. George offered us three bottles of Coca-Cola and wanted to know about our high school and what grade we were in. "Boys" was playing on the radio and John and Paul were listening to it.

Bonnie was recording our conversation on a reel-to-reel that she put in her beach bag she brought in her purse. At the end of the conversation with George suddenly you hear the click of the reel going around and around. And George looked at my girlfriend's purse and looks over to John and Paul and says, "Lads. I believe we've been bugged." And John said, "Did we say anything that would incriminate us?"

Derek comes out, hands us each copies of *Meet The Beatles!* And says, "Ladies, I'm afraid your time is up." Bonnie's father drove down the hill for an hour. He went into a coffee shop and then picked us up.

We didn't go to the Hollywood Bowl 1964 concert.

We thanked George's mother over and over again. We got about five or six letters from Mrs. Harrison. We sent her stuff for Christmas. We went to England in 1965 but they weren't living there anymore.

I saw the Beatles in 1965 at the Hollywood Bowl. At the time I was dating Bobby Fuller. I never met Dave Hull. Now with the KRLA DJ Casey Kasem, we go back. Anytime we had something going on with Bobby all I had to do was pick up the telephone and say, "Casey…" "Just tell me where and when and I'll be there." He was an amazing man. I adore him.

I am now seeing the Beatles in '65 and it's a whole half hour of just them. I enjoyed the show, considering they were six bucks and I remember at one time the screaming got to be so loud. I stood up and yelled, "Shut up! I paid six bucks and I want to hear them!" I remember John coaxing a girl into the pool in front of the stage at the Hollywood Bowl. He knew she was gonna dive into the pool.

A Hard Day's Night didn't blow my mind but it was fun. If this is a day in the life of the Beatles I feel sorry for them. We just went to the box office in Panorama City and got tickets for the movie.

There were some scenes in *Help!* where I was very impressed with George. His acting kind of improved since *A Hard Day's Night*. Ringo, as always, was very good.

When I hear a song they did, especially one they were playing at the house, it's a memory. "I was sitting by the pool with George Harrison." For me, being a Beatles' fan, it's a memory of a lifetime.

In 1965 I saw Derek Taylor again. The Teenage Fair at the Hollywood Palladium. Derek was sitting on top of the KRLA booth with the DJ Dick Biondi. And he looked down, said hello. He remembered us.

In the Nineties I connected with Louise Harrison, George's sister, at a Beatles' convention in Pasadena. I told her the whole story. She just kept on saying, "That was Mum." She said George disapproved of his mother answering the fan mail. He would rather she didn't. But she said, "That was Mum."

It's no secret as to why America and particularly the Southern California basin had a physical and fiscal attraction to this newfound sound. During 1962–1964, the Beatles themselves could almost be considered foreign exchange students from Los Angeles enrolled for a few semesters studying abroad, while simultaneously devising their own L.A. music tribute cover band.

They all had library cards of vinyl, courtesy of the Specialty, Modern, Aladdin, Imperial, Liberty, Dot, Lute, Philles, and Del-Fi branches.

Repertoire visits culled from the Capitol Records wares in Hollywood were certainly heard and not lost on Paul McCartney.

"Till There Was You" was written by Meredith Willson in 1957 for *The Music Man*, a 1962 feature film that was first a cast album recording for Capitol in 1957, produced by Nelson Riddle, before a Broadway run in New York.

The Bakersfield, California–based Buck Owens recorded his "Act Naturally" at the Capitol Records studios in February '63; it had a big impression on Ringo Starr.

At a 2013 press conference to launch his *Ringo Peace & Love* exhibit at the Grammy Museum running to March 2014 in Los Angeles, longtime area resident Ringo Starr told me he might have relocated to the United States years before the Beatles even reached American shores.

Ringo's musical hero was Lightnin' Hopkins, who recorded for the Culver City-based Aladdin Records label in West L.A. When Ringo was age 19, he and a friend were "seriously considering moving to Houston to work in a factory," because they wanted to be close to the blues man.

Ringo also addressed the Beatles and Elvis Presley August 27, 1965 meeting held at Presley's Perugia Way home in Bel-Air.

"We didn't jam with Elvis. I don't care who says it. The big memory was we walked in and Elvis was on the settee watching TV and he had a TV commander (remote) and we were all like, 'Wow!' For us, we were fans of Elvis. When he came in he was just incredible. For me, I was used to seeing people like Bill Haley and a lot of other guys and they all seemed like your dad. And Elvis, for me, was the first one who wasn't like my dad. Those are the big memories. We didn't jam and we didn't really play American football although he and his guys did; we didn't know how to play that."

In 1958, Chan Romero wrote "Hippy Hippy Shake," and his July 1959 record, out on the Hollywood-based Del-Fi label, was widely popular in East Los Angeles. The record, discovered by Paul McCartney, formed a crucial part of most each and every set at Liverpool's Cavern Club and the Star Club in Hamburg, Germany, as an opener or closer.

Lafayette, Louisiana–born and Los Angeles–raised blues guitarist Bobby Parker, who worked with the heralded L.A. legends Don & Dewey and the immortal Sam Cooke as a teenager, had a chart single in 1961 with "Watch Your Step."
During '61 live shows the Beatles would often include his tune. Later, in the documentary *John Lennon's Jukebox*, Lennon would cite Parker's opening guitar riff as inspiring his "I Feel Fine" lead part. In a 1974 WNEW-FM radio interview Lennon mentioned Parker's lick as influencing the beginning of "Day Tripper" as well.
Actress, dancer and singer Ann-Margaret, an RCA Records recording artist, had a *Billboard* Top 20 hit in 1961 with "I Just Don't Understand," later included on one of the Beatles' BBC radio bookings.

"John, Paul, and George first developed their 'This Boy' and 'Yes It Is' three-part harmony to Phil Spector's 'To Know Him Is to Love Him' backstage in Hamburg," confirmed Gary Pig Gold. "Meanwhile, Larry Williams was indeed the savage young Beatles' *second*-favorite Specialty recording artist, and Coasters songs featured prominently in the band's, albeit failed, January 1, 1962, Decca Records audition."

Live at the BBC and the 2013 *On Air—Live at the BBC Volume 2* also reveal their fondness for Spector's "To Know Her Is to Love Her," Romero's "Hippy Hippy Shake," Little Richard's "Lucille" on Specialty, Leiber and Stoller's "Young Blood" and their "Kansas City/Hey, Hey, Hey, Hey" medley, with Williams' "Dizzy Miss Lizzy," "Bad Boy," and "Slow Down." Was not Little Richard's co-written "Long Tall Sally" shouter, a staple of the Beatles' live repertoire in 1963 and '64, also committed to vinyl?

There is also the overtly Walt Disney–inspired "Do You Want to Know a Secret?" A *Billboard* No. 2 single released on Vee-Jay, taken from the *Please Please Me* '63 album, sung by George Harrison, it has its origins in Disney's "I'm Wishing" off the animated 1937 *Snow White* movie, certainly colored this Lennon/McCartney effort.

This song also launched fellow Epstein-managed Liverpudlian Billy J. Kramer's recording career: It was released in April of '63, hitting No. 2 on the U.K. charts, making it the first cover of a Lennon/McCartney composition to become a genuine hit.

Do we even need to mention what discovering the Ken Nelson–produced "Be-Bop-a-Lula" by Gene Vincent on Capitol during 1956 did to John Lennon?

When McCartney saw Lennon with the Quarrymen for the first time in 1957, John was singing (and parodying) the Del-Vikings' "Come Go With Me," a Dot single from the

Vine Street–situated company in Hollywood, distributed in the U.K. by the London label.

Paul consequently auditioned for John's band with his attempt of Eddie Cochran's "Twenty Flight Rock," first recorded in Hollywood at Gold Star Studios in 1956. The Beatles would further turn to the Dot Records catalogue for Arthur Alexander's "Soldier of Love," "A Shot of Rhythm and Blues" and "Anna (Go to Him)."

After the Beatles' 1962 lunchtime sets at the Cavern Club in Liverpool it was Kitty Lester's version of "Love Letters" that was played afternoons inside that venue.

The record was produced by Four Preps member and Hollywood High School graduate Ed Cobb in 1961 for the Era label in Los Angeles, with pianist Lincoln Mayorga and Earl Palmer on drums. As a songwriter, Cobb would later pen the hits "Tainted Love" for Gloria Jones and Soft Cell as well as "Dirty Water" by the Standells.

"When I was the lead guitarist of the Everly Brothers 1961–1963 we rotated nights with the Beatles at the Star Club in Hamburg, Germany," recollected guitarist Don Peake. "John and Paul watched our shows. I always liked the Beatles and I knew they would be successful just like the Rolling Stones, who opened for us on a tour of England in 1963. I'm on the John Lennon *Rock 'n' Roll* album that Phil Spector produced in 1973."

Let's also not forget the fashion influence pop vocalist Chris Montez might have had on the Beatles after their joint 1963 U.K. tour. Their tailor was instructed to make colorless jackets modeled exactly from Montez's wardrobe.

When the Beatles arrived in Hollywood, just before their '64 Hollywood Bowl date, taped by Capitol Records producer Voyle Gilmore, Paul McCartney made a visit to the home of Nik Venet, a trusted friend of Brian Wilson, who signed the Beach Boys to the Capitol label and produced their first two albums.

Even as late as 1967, when the Turtles first came to London on the heels of their hit record "Happy Together," McCartney and the group's Howard Kaylan traded verses one night on Don & Dewey's "Justine" at the Speakeasy Club. Paul "loved the song," and Ringo played the spoons along with them on the tabletop.

The game-changing Jerry Leiber and Mike Stoller songwriting team wrote three songs on the Beatles' *Live at the BBC* set: "Kansas City," "Young Blood" and "Some Other Guy." At the Beatles Decca audition their "Three Cool Cats" was recorded.

The duo's "Some Other Guy" tune, a song Richard Barrett originally did when Leiber and Stoller operated Red Bird Records, was heard on the very early film clip of the Beatles performing at the Cavern. It was the first black-and-white footage America saw of the band.

In 1997, Jerry Leiber and Mike Stoller provided their memories to me in a joint interview.

Mike Stoller: "I heard years ago a tiny bit of "Some Other Guy" at the Cavern, and it had been in a documentary. I could barely hear it.

We were recording Richard. He was involved with the Chantels. He produced them, and I guess he wrote a lot of their songs, I don't remember. He was a very capable producer and writer on his own. He wanted to do a session as an artist. We produced that, and we were going to put it out on our own label, I can't exactly remember what year it was, but we ended up, I think, leasing it to Atlantic. Two sides, that's all we did with him. 'Some Other Guy' and a thing called 'Tricky Dickey,' and I guess it found its way to Liverpool. It was not a hit."

Jerry Leiber: I have no sense of the passage of time and it's like they cut it last night, and someone said, 'You want to hear a Beatles cut?' 'Yeah, great.' I don't have this long sense of distance and time and history and baggage. I don't have it. I think we both experience time and history differently. I think the two of us are in some kinda time warp, because…

Mike Stoller: I'm in time and he's warped…I've never heard the Beatles do "Young Blood." I know Leon Russell did it at the Bangladesh concert.

Jerry Leiber: That's the only song in that whole raft of rhythm & blues, rock 'n' roll songs that was written in this fashion. Jerry Wexler was taking me to his house in his green convertible Cadillac that he was ready to trade in 'cause the bumpers were falling of it. He lived in Great Neck [New York] and his wife Shirley was gonna cook me this great dinner that night. And he was taking me home. On the way down to the garage to get the car, Jerry said, "Doc [Pomus] has this great title and he's having trouble writing. Would you like to take a crack at it?" I was smart but very naïve at the same time. I didn't know I was being hustled into a thing. *[Laughs.]*

Mike Stoller: We were later sitting in Atlantic's recording studio and we were mixing something else and Jerry gave me the song on a legal pad and I wrote the music. I started singing it and that was it. Doc—and this isn't to take anything away from Doc, who was a great writer—Doc wrote the title. We recorded it in Los Angeles. We wrote it in New York. We came to L.A. and had "Young Blood" and wrote three others including "Searchin'" and went to record on Fairfax Avenue.

"I remember that one of the Coasters, one of the original members, was unable to come to the studio that day, so as a ringer we got Young Jessie. And so Young Jessie is one of the voices."

Jerry Leiber: We wrote "Kansas City/Hey! Hey! Hey! Hey!" When we did that with Little Willie Littlefield it was all right. Later, Wilbert Harrison's version came out; it sounded right.

Mike Stoller: Between the Beatles records and Paul McCartney's recordings there is a vast array of versions, but the first version was taken from Little Richard's version, which came out in the U.S. right after Wilbert Harrison's record came out. It just said "Kansas City." Little Richard did the four "hey hey"s.

"I liked Paul McCartney as a vocalist, and especially loved him in those melodic things he wrote. Between him and John Lennon, that was the 1960s as far as I'm concerned. And I loved the way he sang our songs. Beautiful."

Phil Spector was on the February 1964 airplane flight from England that brought the Beatles to America.

In 1961, when Spector was based at Atlantic Records, he co-produced (with Jerry Wexler) the first version of "Twist and Shout," a Bert Berns and Phil Medley song first recorded by the Topnotes.

The next year Berns went into the studio himself and produced it again with the Isley Brothers. The Beatles consequently copied their version from that record. Spector and Wexler were the studio midwives of this often-copied rock anthem.

In 2008, Wexler was more than happy to offer his opinions on Phil Spector.

"He was sleeping on the couch at the Atlantic Records offices when I first met him and had a scam going using the switchboard after hours.

"All of Phil's aggressions and talents were apparent to us at Atlantic when he was a kid. He was brash, cocky and talented. Ahmet Ertegun took him out to L.A. for a business and record meeting with Bobby Darin when Bobby was cruising on the charts. And Phil insulted Bobby, dismissing some of the records. That was Phil. A pop genius like Jerry Leiber.

"I respect Phil," said Wexler. "He could do it all. The song and the recording existed in his brain. Phil's records were made in his head before he even entered the recording studio. When Phil went into the studio, it came out of him, like Minerva coming out of Jupiter's head. Every instrument had its role to play, and it was all prefigured. The singer was just one tile in this intaglio.

"How could I later argue with the results and success when Phil really became a record producer with his Wall of Sound and his studio mesh of instruments? Although I like records with more definition. I'm still very fond of him," lauded Wexler, who authored the liner notes to a mid-'70s Phil Spector International label album, *The Law, Language and Lenny Bruce*.

In 1971 an event was held in West Hollywood inside the Ash Grove club billed as a "Phil Spector Seminar on Today's Recording Industry."

Phil arrived in a Rolls-Royce, wearing a black suit, and addressed the adoring throng. He was using an English accent throughout the orientation when he gave an illuminating music lecture on Melrose Ave., literally 300 yards from the campus of Fairfax High School. Spector later explained his employment of the English accent. "It's only because I've lived in London for the past few years working with the four has-beens," Phil joked.

By 1970, Spector was very involved in the record division of the Beatles' Apple Records and was producing *Let It Be*. Phil discussed the Beatles, and rambled a bit while addressing a question regarding his creative control with the by then disbanded group.

"I had a goodly amount of creative control, but you see, when the Beatles worked together, as four, they bounced off each other. In the realm of *Let It Be*, I practically...I either made it or destroyed it. It's their second largest selling of all time.

"I met the boys, John and all the boys, I met them years and years ago and they used to ask me, 'Phil, how did you make all those consecutive hit records in a row, what'd you do?' I said, 'Well, I listen to everything around. I listen to what I'm making or just made and I'd say if it's better or not, and then I'd put it out and it becomes No. 1.' And they said, 'That's how we made our early albums. That's how we did it.'

"So, while there was a secret to the extent of how it was made, there was no secret to disguise that it's really hard work. I was mainly interested in singles and establishing a reputation in the record business, and they were interested only in making albums, and that's why so much of it that we did was really good, because we listened to what was around us and we compared. And John really left the Beatles long before Paul ever did, because the record I did with John, 'Instant Karma,' came out almost a year before Paul ever made his first solo album. So John Ono Lennon was recording solo long before Paul McCartney. In fact, a great myth about the Beatles was that they wrote together. Well, after '65, they never wrote together."

In my own 1975 *Melody Maker* published interview with Phil done at his Beverly Hills mansion, we discussed the Beatles and John Lennon. Spector spoke about the Crystals' "Then He Kissed Me" and the mid-Sixties instrumental impact it had on the Beatles.

"That was an experimental record," Phil explained over a meal of steak tartar dipped in a jar of mayonnaise. "John told me the Beatles got the idea to use a 12-string guitar from that record. But I thought it was too spaced out. I was against it coming out. I was gonna can it.

"It was very easy to work with John Lennon," Phil confided at the time. "There was no problem working with him. I think he is one of the greatest singers in music. I honestly believe that. I feel the same way about Paul as a singer. They are in a league with few others. I don't feel the same way about George or Ringo. John and Paul are great rock 'n' roll singers."

Before songwriter, record producer and Sirius XM satellite radio DJ Kim Fowley went to England in 1964, just after the Beatles owned the U.S. record charts that year, he heard the Beatles for the first time on KRLA.

"In 1963 I was driving with Danny Hutton on the way to the beach, and the Beatles' 'Please Please Me' came on the radio, and we both said, 'The Everly Brothers with a third harmony part and Carole King and Gerry Goffin melodies. This works!'

"I was with Danny when I saw them on *Ed Sullivan*. It was in West L.A., Pacific Palisades or Brentwood, with some girls and their family watching TV.

"It was four guys dressed alike with the same haircut doing uniformity rock. It was like a miniature army up there. They had catchy songs on television with yelling girls. It was fine. I'd been on TV before and I had also seen crowd bedlam around black R&B shows I was at. But they were white and they had clothing and hair from somewhere else. Some other universe.

"I saw human male dolls for little girls to play with, and their hair, shoes, Beatle boots, clothes, were unique. The whole thing was new. Even though it wasn't new to a lot of people.

"In *Record World* in 1964, the third music trade magazine in the U.S. behind *Billboard* and *Cash Box*, I had just produced the No. 1 hit 'Popsicles and Icicles' by the Murmaids. The next week 'I Want to Hold Your Hand' replaced me. So I figured everybody was knocked out. Only people like Terry Stafford with 'Suspicion,' 'Dawn' by the Four Seasons and Louis Armstrong with 'What a Wonderful World' had hits. So I went to England to learn what it was that caused everything to change. That's all reflex.

"When the Beatles arrived and charted in America, everything became different. One day it changed, just like one day it changed when Elvis Presley arrived. One day it changed when Frank Sinatra arrived. One day it changed when Enrico Caruso arrived. And when Alexander's Ragtime Band arrived. I mean, they are certain musical moments that arrived without notice, and if you were in the industry or the media or the public you dealt with it. Whether you wanted to or not. And you had to co-exist with it and interact with it and rebuild around the change. Just like the horse to the horse-and-buggy and then the locomotive. Black-and-white television turning into color. Same-sex marriage, all those things.

"America and Hollywood in late 1963 was dealing with the loss of John F. Kennedy. When the Beatles took over the charts and AM radio playlists, locally and nationally, I was a guy who had three hit records already. On the day JFK died, I sold 88,000 copies of the Murmaids' 'Popsicles and Icicles.' People were really sad and needed a 45rpm.

"All during 1963 a lot of regional labels passed on the Beatles. The Hollywood and L.A. record companies still had a shirt-and-tie vibe. They really didn't want to let foreigners into their offices.

"Before the Beatles scored big with 'I Want to Hold Your Hand,' I had been at Capitol Records. They were hateful. They hated blacks, they hated browns, and they hated yellows, American Indians, hippies, beatniks, fags, rednecks and lesbians. You came up with a slur, they ram it up your ass. Some of the record executives were very hateful. One came across like a Nazi. They looked down on everything. Nobody cared.

"Record companies always hate the artist, and publishing companies always despise the writer, bartenders always hate the bands, housewives always hate the employees of the husband. It's just a big list of dislikes that go on," sighed Fowley.

"Then in 1964 I was at Dick James Music office in England hustling. They were the Beatles' original music publishers via Northern Songs. Here come the four Beatles in suits with the neckties, and Brian Epstein, their manager, ran in and said, 'Everybody stand up and applaud the boys.' And they walked in the door.

"I met Ringo on two different occasions," Fowley rhapsodizes. "Once in 1964 at the Ad Lib Club when I was introduced to him as the co-producer and co-publisher of 'Alley Oop' by the Hollywood Argyles. He told me that the Beatles recorded my tune 'Alley Oop' at Abbey Road. They did it but it was never mixed down or issued. But it's in the vaults at the studio.

"It was in 1964 when Murray Deutch of the music division from United Artists Records came in, who didn't care about the Beatles' movie *A Hard Day's Night*, they just wanted the soundtrack override. That's what he said to me. Murray had worked with Buddy Holly and now had the James Bond franchise. Mike Stewart of United Artists Records in America got the rights domestically, even though, as you know, the Beatles were on Capitol Records.

Clipping courtesy of Jim Roup

"*A Hard Day's Night* was a big, important moment in the development and the evolution of the rock song in film and the movie soundtrack as a retail item and stand-alone product itself," dictates entertainment business veteran Fowley.

"In 1966 at the Ad Lib Paul McCartney was there, disguised and dressed as an Arab and walking around. I also met him at a party he politely crashed in St. John's Wood down the street from him. Paul saw a bunch of cars parked and he dropped in to take a look, jumped back in his own car and split.

"Also in 1966, I spent some time with John and Paul in London. Bruce Johnston of the Beach Boys was in town doing advance publicity for the Beach Boys' *Pet Sounds* and had an acetate pressing with him. I was asked to bring the Who's Keith Moon over, who brought John and Paul to the hotel room. They were both very impressed by the recording, left the hotel and went into the recording studio the next day and did 'Here, There and Everywhere' for *Revolver*. The both of them were able to digest and gauge the whole essence of *Pet Sounds* in one listening.

"I did meet Brian Epstein once time. It was in an underground garage at a hotel after a party and cars were being brought around. I said, 'What is the secret of the Beatles' success?' And he replied, 'Surround your phenomena with specialists. It's a line in my book, *A Cellarful of Noise*. Why don't you buy it and read it?'

"George Martin was the catalyst for the embryonic dreams of Lennon, McCartney, Starkey and Harrison. Martin was able to consolidate and expand their anticipation. He was a great editor.

"I always liked the northern U.K. artists more than the southern U.K. artists because of the Irish blood that flowed in the veins of Lennon and McCartney. It was the Irish refugee coming across the Irish Sea from Ireland and having children and settling into Liverpool, as a seaport city with an Irish background. Ireland has this tremendous music culture. The most musical nation on earth. I'm Irish, by the way, and I get to say that. I'm an Irish citizen.

"You put that Irish sense of melody, and then you put the black music with Chet Atkins and Eddie Cochran, and you stir it all up and the isolation of Liverpool, that North of Watford situation, where everyone in the South of England thinks they're so sensitive and so brilliant, but all the soul of England is north of Watford, especially in the northern part with Liverpool."

It Was 50 Years Ago Today: The Beatles Invade America and Hollywood

PART 2: LAST SECOND OF A BIG DREAM

Musician Ian Whitcomb is a graduate of Trinity College, Dublin, Ireland, who was born in Surrey, England, and had an American Top 10 piano-infused hit single in 1965 with "You Turn Me On."

He was the original host of the British rock television program *The Old Grey Whistle Test.*

Whitcomb has authored 11 books and is a former KROQ-FM DJ who is now heard weekly on www.luxuriaradio.com as well as hosting the Premiere Network's *Ian Whitcomb Show.* The musicologist currently resides in Pasadena, California, with his singing wife, Regina. In 2012 Whitcomb became a U.S. citizen.

"I just didn't sing but played the piano as well. I'm rooted in Eddie Cochran, Jerry Lee Lewis and George Formby. I then see rock bands writing their own songs. The point that I'm gonna make is that the change came in when songs on their own, songs separately, which anyone could record, went out.

"And the Beatles were the last people to write really well made songs. And they really came up, and I've said this before, they are actually at the end of the well-made popular song. They grew up understanding the form of popular song. The Tin Pan Alley form. They understood it. Lennon and McCartney. They're not actually the spear headers, they're the old guard with it, a last gasp of the well-made song," argues Whitcomb.

Although it must be said that the Elton John and Bernie Taupin songwriting team from 1969 to 1972 might have also continued the Tin Pan Alley tradition. And a 1958 issue of *VARIETY* hailed Eddie Cochran and others as harbingers of the new "singer-songwriter era."

"Now when the whole rot came in," moans Whitcomb, "I witnessed it, in 1964, in Seattle playing in a coffee house. 'Cause I was playing rock 'n' roll with a piano, and even in '64 I realized and recognized the enemy, and the enemy were college students pretending to be bored people. They were the most despicable of them all because they are middle-class well-to-do pretending to be poor. They actually despise the real problem. They're rich kids but they think it's good to dress up and pretend to be the people and pretend to be poor. But then they got guitars as well. They despised rock 'n' roll.

"I was playing in Seattle, 'Why are you playing this commercial trash?' 'Johnny B. Goode' and stuff like that. And they would sing these folk songs. And then the archvillain came in, of course—Mr. Zimmerman and his followers, the worst. He himself I'm sure is a very nice chap. But the point is it's his followers I don't like.

"With his success we had people coming in that despise the well-made song, who despised Tin Pan Alley, and all the stuff the Beach Boys had done, and the Wrecking Crew were schlock. So that's the beginning of the end. 1965, 1966. That's when the decadent middle-class student brigade came in and destroyed rock 'n' roll.

"I liked the Mamas and Papas," he admits, "and they fit in that period before the folkies and the pseudo-folkies who couldn't play came in. They were musicians, and Mama Cass liked the old songs. So she obviously had good taste. She loved the well-made song, the Tin Pan Alley song. John Phillips was a good songwriter and wrote well-made songs.

"Immediately, the new rock people came in—I knew they were the enemy 'cause they disliked me. 'Cause they knew I liked Tin Pan Alley, George Formby, that I thought popular music should be heavily made but appear to be lightweight. And that you were entertaining people, not with your back to the audience.

"I was the first person to bring a piano into Doug Weston's Troubadour club. I became the first rock 'n' roll act. I started off with the old songs, and second half I would do my ragtime stuff on the piano. Doug rented a lovely upright piano. I went down quite well. I was backed by Somebody's Children. Derek Taylor, author Christopher Isherwood, and artists Don Bachardy and David Hockney came to see me."

In an interview with journalist Kirk Silsbee in the August 28, 2003, *L.A. CityBeat*, Little Steven Van Zandt examined the immediate foothold the Beatles had on American soil and a link between England and Los Angeles. Van Zandt hosts a weekly Beatles program on his Sirius XM Underground Garage channel.

"After World War II, everybody moved to the suburbs. In the late '50s, for the first time, teenagers became a demographic with money to spend. Rock 'n' roll captured the imagination in a way that took your mind away from the goal of getting a job and a career. Momentarily, anyway. Rock 'n' roll suggested the possibility of getting a job in rock 'n' roll.

"Before the Beatles, there were no bands, except the Crickets—Buddy Holly's band. On February 13, 1964, there were no bands. On February 14, everybody wanted to start a band.

"I think in many cases L.A. was further ahead culturally—certainly fashion-wise. L.A. may have been further ahead, actually, than the East Coast in some funny way.

There's always been a connection between England and L.A. that seemed to be odd and interesting. More so than England and New York, even though it's so much closer."

"The Beatles changed the game," acknowledges Dino Danelli of hitmakers the Rascals. "I mean, that's the reason we got together. Felix [Cavaliere] and I were in Las Vegas together when the Beatles came over. And we just looked at one another and said, 'Wow. Look at what these guys are doing.' We heard them on the radio before we saw them on *Ed Sullivan*. That was it. We knew. We had just met a little bit previously and wanted to do something together seriously in a band.

"And then here comes these guys. So they were responsible for us to really making the jump and putting the Young Rascals band together. We had an animal name. We wore knickers in the early days. The hair, mop-tops. And the Beatles were leading the way. They understood harmonies and melodies. And from 1964 we were all constantly listening to them. Their influence came into the writing, performing and the recording. They were setting the way for the world.

"And we were just taking their influences on the Rascals and making it our own. We saw them at Shea Stadium in 1965. We were there but it was nothing but screaming. We were in the dugout but couldn't hear a note.

"And I would compare 'How Can I Be Sure' to McCartney's 'Yesterday.' It's classic and gorgeous. Felix wrote one of the most beautiful melodies in a rock situation I can remember. And Arif [Mardin] wrote a beautiful arrangement for it. Everybody just clicked on it. Eddie's performance was outstanding. You could not fight that song."

"The Beatles changed my whole life," volunteers Rascals guitarist Gene Cornish. "Before I heard them or saw them, when I was a guitar player it was to be behind the singer in the background. Las Vegas was maybe one of the places you would end up at. Maybe the guitar player on some tour behind Freddy Cannon. Now, all of a sudden, the Beatles come out and I can walk up front. There were no sidemen in the Beatles. There were no sidemen in the Rascals. There's no sidemen in the Rolling Stones. Or the Who. It was us. I could stand there and wait for my solo. But it wasn't just the solo. I added to the rhythm. We were a four-man team. And then the Beatles wrote their own music. We could sing it and play up front and it wasn't just the lead guy singing up front. It was no longer, 'mind your own business and stay in the back.'"

"The first time I heard 'I Want to Hold Your Hand,' my mother-in-law goes, 'they're called the Beatles. They are the biggest new things in radio,'" howled Brian Wilson during a 2007 lunch encounter in Southern California.

"They didn't scare me but made me jealous. I was so jealous I could have cried. Because they got a lot of attention we didn't get. And I didn't want them to eclipse the Beach Boys, so to speak.

"Listening to music on pot, I got more into it than usual. Well, when I first took it, I listened to *Rubber Soul* and then I went to the piano and all I could see were my keys. Only the keyboard and I locked in with it and wrote 'God Only Knows.'

"I watched *The Beatles Anthology* on television and it was an awful lot of music to take in one night! I got sad at the end of the program when they were breaking up. 'All My Loving' and 'Michelle' are my two favorite Paul bass lines. Paul's song 'Let It Be' saved many bad nights of mine when I was going through a really rough trip and 'Let It Be' would come right to me. Out of nowhere. It healed me. I would call

Paul McCartney a very wonderful singer. I love Paul's 'The Long and Winding Road' because of the chord structure and the message. My favorite John Lennon song is 'Across the Universe.' I also love 'Because.'

"One of the guitar leads on 'Marcella' was inspired by George Harrison. Absolutely. Marcella was a Spanish chick that worked at a local massage parlor. I love George Martin's production work. The horn arrangement is very humorous on 'All You Need Is Love.'

"John Lennon and Paul McCartney as songwriters—they are amazing. Well, there's no way they've ever sounded better than that theater in Las Vegas at the Mirage Hotel for *LOVE*. I'll tell you that right now. I thought it was one of the most brilliant pieces of music production I have ever heard in my entire life!

"I went there thinking it was going to be some look-alike Beatles guys, a tribute thing. What! A totally different show! I wasn't ready! What it did to me was make me so very proud of the Beatles. The sound of that theater probably couldn't be equaled by any place anywhere in the world. I now realized about the sound that I heard something that was a manifestation of a very, very good-natured person like Giles Martin. A very good sense of humor. You gotta see it. Seeing it made me more proud than ever of the Beatles. It made me realize how great they were with music. I could not believe how good Ringo's drums sounded! I could not believe it. It was dynamic. You will not believe it. You got to go and see *LOVE*. Take your chick! You'll be glad you did. I saw it a second time."

"It was the early sixties... I just returned from one year in London and Europe," spiels Dennis Dragon, the Surf Punks' co-founder, record producer and award-winning engineer and studio owner.

"My father, Carmen Dragon, did a stint as guest conductor for the London Philharmonic and the family, minus my oldest brother Doug, went along for the ride. The family was now back living in Malibu, California and Doug and my other brother Daryl and I formed an instrumental trio called the Dragons that played parties and such around the Southern California area. I remember that our musically supportive dad had arranged for the group to record some demos at Capitol Records in Hollywood where he was signed, with the hopes of procuring a record deal for us. At that time, instrumental hit records were commonplace.

"Anyway, the demo was recorded with drummer Hal Blaine, who had just blown into town, on drums, and our friend Ed Carter on Fender bass. My dad, the producer, made the decision to use Hal due to my limited studio experience and young age. The demo, featuring Doug on piano and Daryl on vibes and melodica, turned out great and we were signed to a one-single deal! The 45 that I played drums on was titled 'Elephant Stomp' backed with 'The Troll' and we were off and running. The single received mild airplay here and there, but then something happened. Capitol signed a British group by the name of 'the Beatles' and we were shelved. Instrumentals were forgotten and vocals were the way to go. The Dragons faded into obscurity..."

"We'd sometimes play the Troubadour in Hollywood for a week or two weeks in a row," remembers the MFQ's Henry Diltz. "And *A Hard Day's Night* was billed at an all-night movie theater on Hollywood Boulevard. There were two houses on Hollywood Boulevard that had double features and open to 4:00 am. We went to a screening after a Troubadour show. I had a little reel-to-reel tape recorder, and I sneaked it in under my coat and sat it on my lap and recorded the whole soundtrack to *A Hard Day's Night*. 'Cause I wanted to also hear the dialogue with the songs. I went back and saw it a second time."

The Beefeaters -- 1964
photo by Jim Dickson/Henry Diltz Archives

"It was around the time I first met Gene Clark. I was at the Troubadour one night when they had tables near the bar. And there was my friend David Crosby and Jim McGuinn, with another guy. 'Hey Tad. Meet our new friend Gene Clark. He just moved here from St. Louis and we're going to start a group and call it the Beefeaters.' I went, 'Oh man, that's great.' I was Tad at the time, and changed my name, like Jim later did to Roger, from our belief in Subud. They loved the Beatles, and McGuinn would get up on stage at the Troubadour hoot nights and do Beatles songs solo on a Rickenbacker. I sent my girlfriend Alexa in Hawaii a letter about the MFQ in Hollywood and the new Beefeaters group.

Part 2: Last Second of a Big Dream

> mfg
>
> Dear Alexa,
>
> See what I bought at Farmer's Market yesterday? We took TR there for a sight-seeing shopping trip. He was just here one day and now he is back in Honolulu.
>
> About all we've done so far is sit around the Tropicana practicing and listening to Jim McGuinn, Dave Crosby, and another chap (Gene Clark) sing their newly arranged (and written) Beatles-type songs. They are very good and stand a good chance of selling a lot of records.
>
> Also, we have been to see "Hard Day's Night" (Beatles movie x-us if you didn't know) two nights in a row. Obviously we liked it! and tonight we sang at Disneyland. It was a very good audience and we had a lot of fun and so did they. We sing there again tomorrow night.
>
> The Troubador has really become a camp for the Men... like a Boy Scout training camp or a Peace Corps Stud Farm Boot Camp... with pep talk meetings hourly (day and night) mimeographed memos and "Women Behind the Men" register table in the lobby. retch!

"In 1965 I was living in Laurel Canyon. We were taking LSD one evening—it was legal then, and on occasion would do it on a weekend. I did it maybe 12 times in my life. But I always thought that acid was a good time to reflect and meditate. And really learn from it. So we took it with my friends in my little one-room studio apartment on Rosella Place. The other people then started to do the social thing on LSD, laugh and tell stories, and just kind of party. I don't do that. So I decided to go outside and walk up the hill, and I could see across Laurel Canyon. I started to meditate and I could hear these mosquitos around me. I didn't want them to bite me. So I granted them 'being.' They had as much right to be here as me. 'I grant you being, but just don't bite me, little brothers.'

"Then I hear this magical music wafting through the air. It was delicate but a fantastic sound drawing me to a house. And I had to get up and follow it. I went down the hill and across the street like you follow the scent of a cherry pie on a windowsill. And I arrived at this little house across the street where Cynthia Webb lived. She was a go-go dancer. A beautiful black lady that I knew very well. I saw her inside and tapped on her door and she was very gracious and invited me in. I was tripping. And she sat me down right in the middle of this circle of candles in little glasses. And then this music was playing. The Beatles' *Rubber Soul.* Cynthia had an advance copy of it from Chris Hillman of the Byrds, who brought it back from England. She showed me the LP cover. The photo bends; it's like an acid picture.

"And Cynthia would eventually marry the artist and musician, Klaus Voormann, who designed the front cover of *Revolver.*

"In summer of 1966, I went with the Lovin' Spoonful to see the Beatles at Shea Stadium in New York. We had seats on the side bleachers, and they were popular in their own right. So dig this. They all go in disguise with hoods, one guy with a cowboy hat and sunglasses. And they go so heavily in disguise they had to be somebody famous. And pretty soon, as they are sitting in their seats, interest starts mounting from the girls around them as the stands get fuller. Everyone is on a hair trigger 'cause the Beatles are gonna be there.

"Girls started running over and screaming, 'It's the Beatles!' Somebody on the field said, 'This way!' So the four of them and myself jump over into the fields, and we're directed into a dugout and go through a series of little tunnels on *A Hard Day's Night* level. And we keep running until the guy says, 'In there.' And we walk in, the door closes, and we're in a little dressing room with the four Beatles and that's all. McCartney was playing his bass with a harmonica in his mouth unplugged. Ringo was sitting at a table at one side of the room. Lennon was there. George was on the other side. John Sebastian went and talked to George. I kind of ended up talking to Ringo. I asked him about the stuffed animals that are tossed on stage. 'I take 'em home to me son.' I later told Paul and Ringo the story," affirms Henry.

"As for the still ongoing impact of the Beatles' music, it doesn't seem that long ago. It's on the continuum of our lives. Of my life. It was when I was a musician and on my way in the Sixties, and that was a big part of my trip. Then I kind of segued from music to photography, but it wasn't that long ago. They changed the whole concept of music and recordings. They put so much joy into it. The songs were great and they wrote them. At the time rock 'n' roll bands didn't write their own material. Or folk groups doing all originals. Except for Bob Dylan in 1962.

"The Beatles grew along with their peers," illuminates Henry. "They grew along with all of us, but they kind of presented certain facets of life through their music. But they had put in all this time woodshedding in Germany, like the MFQ had done at the Action club in Hollywood. When a group can play a club night after night, week after week, month after month, you get very tight.

"The MFQ eventually covered 'Run for Your Life.' I sang lead. Years later we also sang 'Yesterday' in four-part harmony.

"The Beatles also had Brian Epstein as their manager. A real advocate of their music. In October of 2013 I spoke at the Genesis Publications party for Ringo's new *Photograph* book in Hollywood. I have a signed copy. There's a reproduction of a memo from Epstein to all the boys. '8:00 pm is the show. Be there at 6:30. Be sure to wear some good clothes. This is important. You've got to really deliver tonight.' He had a little pep talk line in each of the itineraries.

"One day I got a call in 1989 from Ringo to photograph his All-Starr Band. I asked him if I could stand on the stage as his band played for close-ups. He said, 'I'm the drummer, you're the photographer, it's as simple as that.' So subsequently for years I would photograph his groups. That was always our motto. I just shot his 2013 band."

"When the Beatles first came on the scene I was not listening to much rock 'n' roll," confesses multi-instrumentalist Chris Darrow. "I was going to school full time, playing bluegrass at Disneyland and clubs around Los Angeles and was tuning in to mainly country and bluegrass radio. The early-Sixties pop music had turned me away from Top 40 radio, because most of it was stuff I just couldn't handle. My personal record collection was quite extensive, going back to Elvis, Jerry Lee and Chuck Berry, but over the later years I was buying more and more folk and blues albums and especially bluegrass and old-timey music.

"I had heard of the Beatles but it wasn't until I was driving in my 1958 VW bug, painted a metallic, chocolate brown, that I first heard their music. My future wife, Donna, and I were driving down the freeway on our way to the beach when I turned on the radio. The dial was set to KFWB and the first sound that came out of the speakers was 'I Want to Hold Your Hand.' I instantly said to Donna, 'That must be the Beatles. I get it! It's Buddy Holly, the Everly Brothers and high bluegrass harmonies.'

"At that instant I got what they were doing and realized how much of our own American music had been fused together to create their sound. The Beatles and the English Invasion affected a great many of us folk and bluegrass musicians to turn to electric music, wanting to answer back these wannabe Americans by blending our own sensibilities with classic rock 'n' roll. Folk rock.

"Most of the West Coast bands like the Byrds, the Dead, Jefferson Airplane, Moby Grape, and our band,

Kaleidoscope, evolved from folk and bluegrass musicians such as Jerry Garcia, Grace Slick, Chris Hillman and Peter Lewis," underlines Darrow.

"Soon after I heard what was going on in England, I formed my own electric band called the Floggs, yet still had my own bluegrass band as well. That's when I first started really writing songs and thinking that we could do something here in America that could be our version of what was being done in England.

"The change was almost instantaneous, and soon there was a worldwide movement that took over popular music. In 1967 while playing at the Berkeley Folk Festival with Kaleidoscope, I met my best friend, Bob Siggins, a member of a Boston bluegrass band, the Charles River Valley Boys. Their album called *Beatle Country* was my favorite record at the time and was bluegrass covers of Beatle songs. Produced by Paul Rothchild, producer of the Doors and Janis Joplin, the album showed how the Beatles' music was so American in concept. Bluegrass had always been performed with American traditional songs or compositions. This album changed the face of what could be done in that genre. And now bluegrass hosts songs from many diverse sources.

"Later on, while in the Kaleidoscope, our producer, Barry Friedman, who is credited with putting together the Buffalo Springfield and produced works by Paul Butterfield, Nico, the Holy Modal Rounders and Koerner, Ray and Glover, asked me to accompany him to visit local DJ, B. Mitchel Reed. Barry, who later changed his name to, Frazier Mohawk, said he had a surprise for me waiting at BMR's house in Laurel Canyon. Reed, a DJ on the great alternative FM radio station KPPC, had something he wanted to play for us. A friend, who he wouldn't name, had given him a bootleg tape that he wanted to play for us. It was a new album that was about to be released, by none other than the Beatles. This was very top secret and no one had a copy of this. The album was *Sgt. Pepper's Lonely Hearts Club Band.* We were, aside from insiders, a few who got to hear this album before it was officially released.

"I had always wanted to meet the members of the Beatles but there never seemed to be any opportunity in my life to realize this," wished Darrow. "One day I was at United Artists Records on Sunset Boulevard, visiting a friend in the A&R department. While wandering around the building, I passed by one of the lawyer's offices and looked in to see a familiar face. It was someone I would have recognized anywhere but he was smaller in stature than I would have thought. It was John Lennon and he was visiting the office of his lawyer and accompanied by his female companion, May Pang.

"I was invited in and had a chance to meet my favorite Beatle and shake his hand. He was a very nice guy, and a bit shy. I happened to be at the Troubadour the infamous night that he and Harry Nilsson were kicked out of the club for heckling the Smothers Brothers, though I didn't see it happen."

"The Beatles toured Australia in 1964—mass hysteria and every hack Aussie disc jockey trying to ride on their coattails," delineates Melbourne-based writer Michael Macdonald. "The Beatles changed the rules for Aussie bands, who prior to the Beatles were covering '50s rock 'n' roll and doing surf instrumentals. Aussie combos began to grow their hair, wear sharp black suits and Cuban-heeled boots. Motown and R&B in their set lists. Billy Thorpe & the Aztecs and Ray Brown & the Whispers were probably the best Down Under bands that learned from the Beatles.

"By the late '60s, American grooves were leaking into Australia—the Byrds, the Band, Butterfield Blues Band,

Dylan and the soundscapes changed again. Was a pretty cool time really."

"In Hollywood in August of 1964 I was one of the very few people with long hair on Sunset Boulevard," chortles Robert Marchese, the former longtime (1970–1980) manager of Doug Weston's Troubadour and an award-winning record producer of Richard Pryor's live recordings.

"I knew Elmer Valentine, who owned the Whisky a Go Go, and he called me and said the Beatles were coming by his club to see Johnny Rivers and he knew it was gonna be crazy. Elmer paid me and two other guys from England with long hair to dress up in suits like the Beatles and pull up in front of the Whisky in a car so the Beatles could run in through the back door. We were a decoy and got mobbed in the front so some of the band members could get into the club. Crazed chicks who I thought were gonna kill us. Not so much that we got mobbed but when they found out we weren't them. The limo driver pulled us back in and off we went.

"Then in 1965 the Rolling Stones returned to town and they jammed one night at the Action club. It looked like 10,000 people had long hair. I said to myself, 'Jesus Christ. All of these people had been hiding.' They came out of the woodwork. Musicians and artists like Wallace Berman. It was crazy. I was stunned. 'Now it's time for the revolution, I guess.' We took all this shit from everybody for having long hair and digging the Beatles and the Stones, and now the cat was out of the bag.

"I went to the 1964 Beatles Hollywood Bowl," he fondly reminisces. "All the KRLA DJs jointly introduced them from the stage. I was sitting in reserved box seats in front of the pond. Same seats I had in 1968 when I saw Jimi Hendrix and sat with Dave Mason.

It Was 50 Years Ago Today: The Beatles Invade America and Hollywood

THE BEATLES RETURN! HOLLYWOOD BOWL AUGUST 29 - 30

Radio Station KRLA and Bob Eubanks Proudly Present Two Concerts By The Fabulous Beatles AT HOLLYWOOD BOWL AUG. 29, 30

Tickets are available by mail **only**. Applications will be filled by date of receipt. No ticket applications accepted before May 8.
1. No more than six tickets to any one person.
2. Tickets are $3, $4, $5, $6 and $7.
3. A self-addressed, stamped envelope must be included with your order.
4. Tickets will be mailed July 15.
5. If tickets are not available at the price you order, you will be sent tickets for the alternate date. If tickets at that price are not available for either date, you will be sent tickets at the next lowest price, along with a refund.

MAIL TO:

HOLLYWOOD BOWL
P.O. BOX 1951
LOS ANGELES, CALIF., 90028

ON OR AFTER MAY 8

TICKET APPLICATION

I have enclosed a check or money order (NO CASH) payable to HOLLYWOOD BOWL, plus a self-addressed, stamped envelope. Please send me the following BEATLE TICKETS.

☐ 1 TICKET   ☐ $3.00   ☐ AUGUST 29
☐ 2 TICKETS   ☐ $4.00   ☐ AUGUST 30
☐ 3 TICKETS   ☐ $5.00
☐ 4 TICKETS   ☐ $6.00
☐ 5 TICKETS   ☐ $7.00
☐ 6 TICKETS

SEND TO .....
ADDRESS .....
TELEPHONE NO. .....
CITY ..... STATE ..... Zip Code .....

Newspaper announcement courtesy of Gary Strobl Achives

"The Beatles had this aura about them. And L.A. and Hollywood were Beatle towns. That and the Rolling Stones. In 1964 when the Beatles invaded America I knew it was the step after Elvis. Until the Beatles arrived in Hollywood, the record business was Frank Sinatra. It changed quickly. Sunset Boulevard and then the hippies.

"The Beatles and Brian Epstein also had PR guru Derek Taylor. Great guy. Bright man. His media acumen and contacts with the newspapers and key AM radio station in the Los Angeles area were very important in positioning the Beatles locally which planted seeds nationally. Derek gave the scoops to DJs like Dave Hull at KRLA and knew the other British DJs in town like KFWB's Lord Tim, Tommy Vance on KHJ and Dave Diamond and Humble Harve at KBLA.

"L.A. and Hollywood was the epicenter in the U.S. for Beatles activities. We know it started in Hollywood and spread to New York and all over the country. Plenty of great musical shit always began in Hollywood and L.A. The Beatles

Part 2: Last Second of a Big Dream

held press conferences inside the Capitol Records building. George, Paul and Ringo then end up owning houses in the Los Angeles area."

"I had ushered at the Hollywood Bowl for 2 years before the Beatles arrived in the summer of 1964, but nothing prepared me for the feverish insanity of that night," submitted Lanny Waggoner. "Every rumor that they had at last arrived backstage sent screaming ripples across the box seats.

"When a helicopter landed on a nearby hillside, shouts of 'They're here!' exploded into the air.

The atmosphere was so electric that when they finally came on, opening with a monster like 'Twist and Shout' seemed almost cruel. A girl wearing a skirt (!) tried to hurdle the restraining rope I was holding. Despite the sustained shrieking, I could hear the music fine. The most common shout? 'George!'"

KHJ'S "BOSS 30" RECORDS IN SOUTHERN CALIFORNIA!

ISSUE NO. 25 — EFFECTIVE DECEMBER 22, 1965

Last Week	This Week	TITLE	ARTIST	LABEL	Weeks On Survey
(2)	1.	WE CAN WORK IT OUT / DAY TRIPPER	Beatles	Capitol	3
(11)	2.	LIGHTIN' STRIKES	Lou Christie	MGM	3
(3)	3.	LET'S HANG ON	The Four Seasons	Philips	9
(1)	4.	FLOWERS ON THE WALL	The Statler Bros.	Columbia	6
(5)	5.	SOUNDS OF SILENCE	Simon & Garfunkel	Columbia	4
(8)	6.	RUN, BABY RUN	The Newbeats	Hickory	6
(4)	7.	LIES	The Knickerbockers	Challenge	7
(12)	8.	HOLE IN THE WALL	The Packers	Pure Soul Mu.	5
(7)	9.	YOU DIDN'T HAVE TO BE SO NICE	The Lovin' Spoonful	Kama Sutra	6
(9)	10.	EBB TIDE	The Righteous Bros.	Philles	6
(14)	11.	SHE'S JUST MY STYLE	Gary Lewis & The Playboys	Liberty	4
(6)	11.	IT'S MY LIFE	The Animals	MGM	6
(18)	12.	I FOUGHT THE LAW	Bobby Fuller Four	Mustang	3
(26)	13.	THE DUCK	Jackie Lee	Mirwood	4
(23)	14.	JENNY TAKE A RIDE	Mitch Ryder	New Voice	4
(13)	15.	I WILL	Dean Martin	Reprise	4
(16)	16.	A YOUNG GIRL	Noel Harrison	London	3
(15)	17.	I GOT YOU	James Brown	King	8
(17)	18.	ENGLAND SWINGS	Roger Miller	Smash	4
(27)	19.	NO MATTER WHAT SHAPE (YOUR STOMACH'S IN)	T Bones	Liberty	2
(30)	20.	AS TEARS GO BY	The Rolling Stones	London	2
(21)	21.	HANG ON SLOOPY	The Ramsey Lewis Trio	Cadet	7
(10)	22.	I HEAR A SYMPHONY	The Supremes	Motown	10
(20)	23.	OVER AND OVER	Dave Clark Five	Epic	6
(24)	24.	I CAN NEVER GO HOME ANYMORE	Shangri-Las	Red Bird	7
(25)	25.	I SEE THE LIGHT	The Five Americans	Hanna Barbera	2
(28)	26.	MY LOVE	Petula Clark	Warner Bros.	2
(—)	27.	UPTIGHT	Stevie Wonder	Tamla	1
(29)	28.	A MUST TO AVOID	Herman's Hermits	MGM	2
(28)	29.	MAKE THE WORLD GO AWAY	Eddy Arnold	RCA Victor	2
(—)	30.	MEN IN MY LITTLE GIRL'S LIFE	Mike Douglas	Epic	1

KHJ "Boss 30" Chart courtesy of Ray Randolph

It Was 50 Years Ago Today: The Beatles Invade America and Hollywood

Kenneth Kubernik: A Beatles Memory

"1964—that was the year that transformed an earnest, nine-year-old Sherman, puny, scratchy-kneed, into a resolute horn-rimmed Mr. Peabody, driven into a life of resolute mindfulness and restless musical enthusiasms by a confluence of sonic booms which came to define the chalklines of my life and times. I had already adopted some vaguely transgressive poses—preferring LPs to singles, the AFL to the NFL, Vernors to Pepsi—and prided myself on entertaining deep thoughts, even if they were cribbed from Rod Serling's twilight musings.

"Hollywood, or thereabouts, was home, a galaxy of stars choking under blue-brown skies. It was buzzy to be near celebrity, but the thrill wore off after one too many field trips to a studio soundstage—the cool contours of the "Sea View" revealed themselves to be as cheap and phony as anything devised by Potemkin. The seeds of a cynical sod may well have taken root at this time.

"There were, however, rumblings that a strange and unknowable entrancement was about to descend upon our hungering generation. Like massing tribes at a war council, we gathered before our black-and-white TV sets on February 9 and waited for the rapture. I had spent the previous couple of hours at a nearby park playing caroms with gleeful mastery, a rare instance of my predatory drive coming to surface. But I never lost track of the time and was firmly situated in the family den when the fabled waxwork master of ceremonies intoned: 'Here they are—the Beatles!' Walter Cronkite could have interrupted with news about the Martians landing and no one would have paid him the least mind. No, this was the real shot heard 'round the world, something so magnificently fresh yet gratifyingly familiar, so utterly transformative yet perfectly in tune with the moment.

Part 2: Last Second of a Big Dream

"The Beatles' performance packed the biggest punch in showbiz history, and all we felt was a rousing bliss, a harmonious balm which soothed a nation's shattered soul while rejoicing in the prospects of a bright tomorrow. The Beatles sailed to America's shores on the backs of Fats Domino and Chuck Berry, Carl Perkins and the Everly Brothers. They appropriated the best of our country's character and repackaged it to a Mersey backbeat. Putting a man on the moon by decade's end would need nothing more than a sea-to-shining-sea chorus of 'yeah, yeah, yeah.'

"My clearest memory of those magic moments is not their television appearance so much as the reaction in school the following day. Gathered in the playground before class, it was as if everyone had just shared their first kiss with the boy/girl of their heart's desire. Life never felt so good; it would be a hard act to follow.

So many of my other heroes-to-be collided in Los Angeles in 1964. Glenn Gould, Canada's most sublime variation, performed his last concert on April 10 at the Wilshire Ebell Theatre. Later that summer—September 4— saxophonist Wayne Shorter debuted at the Hollywood Bowl with the Miles Davis Quintet, and a new direction in jazz was forged. And in October, the Santa Monica Civic Auditorium played host to the legendary *T.A.M.I. Show*, featuring that jagged riposte to the cuddly Fabs—the lurid Rolling Stones. It was, as Mr. Sinatra sang, a very good year.

"One day, sometime around 1994-95, I got a call from a family friend, a realtor, who had a listing on one of the so-called "Bird" streets high in the Hollywood Hills. She knew I was a pop music enthusiast (ya think?) and that this property—on Blue Jay Way—held some particular cultural cachet. Did I want to come up? I cut her off with a 'Hell yes!' and zoomed off toward Sunset Boulevard with visions of low-lying fog gripping L.A. Imagine my astonishment to be suddenly touring the home George had rented all those years ago, waiting for friends while coaxing a forlorn chord from the Hammond harmonium nestled unobtrusively in the living room. It was still there, and it still played, and my mind caromed off the walls as the world went round and round and round."

In January 2012, Dr. James Cushing, the father of a 30-year-old daughter named Iris, waxed eloquent about the initial February 1964 impressions the Beatles cast over America.

"I begin with the poetic notion that the ritual reappearance of a Dionysian hero—young, sexy, full of vitality and signaling the return of spring—was key to the deeper meaning of JFK, and the reason so many people (women especially) loved him despite his political ineffectiveness as president.

"He had hair, he had erotic charisma, he had TV stardom and a great voice—and then, as it must with all Dionysus stories, tragedy struck. Author Don DeLillo wrote that Dallas 'broke the back of the American Century.' End of this Dionysus cycle? Apparently so...and then, seemingly out of nowhere (Liverpool?), on *The Ed Sullivan Show*, two months and two weeks after November 22, 1963, on the same TV that gave you JFK, we get—who could have predicted it?—four Dionysian heroes who wear the garb of the singer Orpheus!

"My God, the hand of fate traded Kennedy for the Beatles! And so they blended Dionysian ecstatic energy with Orpheus' romantic loyalty to Eurydice for an erotically unbeatable moment."

Dr. Cushing has further concepts on why America welcomed the Beatles' records into the country and onto its airwaves and why they had a riveting impact on pop culture.

"It was a period post–Dwight Eisenhower and now post–John F. Kennedy. America was still in mourning for John F. Kennedy, and we were all still feeling freaked out about the Russians on a Bay of Pigs level. Plus, the whole question about civil rights and civil rights for Negroes were still a bunch of big issues.

"Everything on the news was challenging. Everything was tragic and everything was a bummer. And the postwar period had been primarily one of anxiety and conformity, with a few interesting rebels that stood out, like Allen Ginsberg and Elvis Presley.

"It was the reality that now we had something positive and enthusiastic. Something that gave a kind of grand permission to let all those bottled repressed feelings out. Here was permission to shake your hair, scream and go crazy. There was a sense of tremendous cool, positive energy, tremendous potential for excitement, tremendous permission. Everything about the joy of romance that can happen in public was happening there with the Beatles.

"The girls who went to the Ed Sullivan Theater or the Washington Coliseum or the Hollywood Bowl or Shea Stadium were not going to hear a concert of popular music but to worship an ancient hairy deity in its four-bodied form. Their screams are so loud because years of sexual frustration lie behind them. In looking at footage from this period, it's the girls who are most compelling as they shatter into ecstasy while the boys smile and maintain Olympian cool."

A MOTOWN MEMORY

Motown founder and Jobete Music publisher Berry Gordy Jr. had been in negotiations in early 1964 concerning three Jobete copyrights earmarked for the second U. S. Beatles long player. EMI and Capitol executives were pressuring Gordy for a discount rate of two cents a track, a lower fee at the time; standard was two and three quarters per track. Berry Gordy was not going to budge.

Gordy had met Brian Epstein before that when he visited Hitsville in Detroit. A Beatles business representative was seeking a reduced rate for his Jobete-controlled copyrights earmarked for the Beatles' album.

The group covered Barrett Strong's "Money (That's What I Want)," the Miracles' "You've Really Got a Hold on Me," and "Please Mr. Postman," first done by the Marvelettes.

In my 1997 published interview with Gordy for *HITS* and *Goldmine* magazine inside his Bel-Air mansion, I wanted to know about this 1964 *High Noon*–type showdown duel he had been in. Gordy's coveted signature would allow the pending LP to ship to eager record shops and retail accounts.

After he discussed with his father, Pops Gordy, the midnight demand for a final licensing agreement, Berry Gordy reluctantly accepted the lesser percentages for his prized Jobete jewels. All to the welcome relief of the Brian Epstein office, and especially EMI/Capitol label staffers, who already had pressed 100,000 units of the disc now sitting in a warehouse for rack jobbers and distributors to quickly stock all over America.

"I think there was some guy there doing his job, trying to get rates on whatever they were doing," said Gordy. "They were doing more than one song. If it had been one song, I could say to them, 'You're doing one song.' But you're doing three songs on *The Beatles' Second Album*, and it's negotiating, like when you go to the supermarket and you buy more than one thing, you get a deal. So I thought it was business, and I say it in the book. I never jump on issues as racial unless they really are. Somebody was doing their job on behalf of the Beatles.

"I chuckle, even today. I say it in there [in his book *To Be Loved*]. It's funny, and if I had to do it all over again [accept a discount rate on the three Jobete copyrights] I would make the same decision. It's better to have a part of something than all of nothing," imparts Gordy.

"And when *The Beatles' Second Album* had three of our songs, it just indicated to us that they obviously had been listening to our music and they were aware of it, enjoying it and loving it. It's always been very important to me.

"As far as the U.K. is concerned, it is very, very special to me. Because, actually, we were, I think, more popular there than we were in our own country, you know, for a long time, it seemed. I think the appreciation was different. They were not blasé about our music early on. Way back, the pirate ships and all that stuff, they discovered the sound and they were always very important to me when I'd go over there.

"They were just together. I loved their creativity with what they did with our album covers and how they just did it. And when we first went over there with the fan clubs, and the signs and stuff that they had for us.

"So the U.K. has always been special for Tamla-Motown. I was really busy creating, producing, working with writers and stuff like that. There's a lot of those unsung heroes that set up things for me. I could take credit for being mainly responsible for the product, but a lot of these deals and things were started with people at [distributor] Oriole."

In November 1974 for *Melody Maker* I interviewed Bobby Rogers, a member of the immortal Miracles, and a Tamla-Motown fixture since their inception in 1958, when he joined up with his sister Claudette, Ronnie White, Pete Moore, and William "Smokey" Robinson. Bobby and I were in a Hollywood recording studio, and I probed him about the Beatles.

"I really loved touring with the English groups, back in 1963 and 1964. We used to tour with the Rolling Stones and people like Georgie Fame. During the breaks from touring, a lot of the groups would ask questions about certain songs on our albums.

"Man, those early tours were a trip. Endless hours of bus rides and all these skinny English dudes asking us about the Tamla-Motown sound. Like that blond boy [Brian Jones]. I never realized how important or influential we were on groups like the Stones and Beatles. He said his name was George [Harrison] and he was in a group named the Beatles. We used to party with all the groups, and have become good friends.

"The Miracles have always to this point been a singles-orientated group. Smokey was writing for the group and everybody else. Smokey never really had the opportunity to do a concept thing.

"The best thing that ever happened to music has got to be the *What's Going On* album by Marvin Gaye. Marvin was listening to everything that was around. Beatles, Stones, pop, jazz, etc. You know that *Sgt. Pepper* LP? It was always on Marvin's turntable," revealed Rogers, who is himself heard on the "What's Going On" title vocal track.

"I can't remember whether it was mono or stereo that I first heard the Beatles, I just know that it was different and it was good," touts native Angelino and drummer Paul Body. "I first heard them on KRLA or KFWB, I think in the middle of 1963.

"The song 'From Me To You' was pick of the week or something like that. I remember that it sounded kind of neat. Remember, this was a time that nothing was happening on the teenage channels. You had to go down the dial to KGFJ to get the real deal!" he exclaims.

"'From Me To You' was quickly forgotten and then a few months later in the fall, there they were in *Newsweek*, a whole article about them. By now they were huge in England. It was the first time that I got to see the hairdos and see in print the name Ringo Starr, which sounded like a gunfighter's name. I was beginning to get intrigued.

"Then Kennedy was killed, the country was plunged into a major depression. 'I Want to Hold Your Hand' came out after that, I dug it. It was being played all over the radio. Then there was that little clip on *The Jack Paar Show* around New Year's Eve—*wow*. They were something. That was the first time I ever heard 'She Loves You.' The pump was being primed.

"Then came February 9, 1964. The world sort of changed that night. I remember that a cat named Kenny Smith had the Beatles' album before anybody else, and we played it in music class. It sounded pretty good. Don't know if it was stereo or mono but it was damn fine.

"So from 1964, they have been in our DNA, never would have thought something like that back in 1963. For some reason they had something that Cliff Richard, Tommy Steele and Adam Faith didn't have. For some reason they captured our imagination and have never let go.

"As great as they were and are, I still have go down the dial to dig some Garnet Mimms and Enchanters, the Impressions, Bobby 'Blue' Bland, James, Motown, Stax and all of the other stuff that was played on KGFJ. That stuff has stood the test of time too—mono or stereo, it doesn't matter, because it rocked and it meant something. So did those Liverpool lads. What a glorious time to live in the same time as the Beatles and Willie Mays."

Two months after the Beatles were off the *Sullivan* screen, and after the assault on our senses, came *The Beatles' Second Album*, the second LP for Capitol Records, and their third long player compiled for the United States, following a Vee-Jay Records product, *Introducing...The Beatles*.

"I think that it's complexly tied in with race and class," ponders Dr. Cushing. "'Cause the covers that the Beatles were doing, in almost every case, as Paul McCartney said at a press conference, 'colored American groups.' In other words, it was white people doing black music. Renditions of Berry Gordy Jr.'s Motown label records. But it was nothing like Pat Boone de-clawing Little Richard. If anything, the Beatles were adding their own muscle to it.

"Lennon and McCartney would perform these critical deconstructions of American popular music, and what changed was the scope of their ambition," observes Dr. Cushing. "McCartney has said that all the early songs had lyrics like spoke to a very limited range. 'Me, you, we, she loves you.' But there was a kind of protected intimacy to them. And as they grew as writers, they grew to take more and more of the larger world as their subject. Until with things like 'A Day in the Life' and 'I Am the Walrus.'

"George Martin was the real fifth Beatles in terms of making the music happen. Their work still holds up because of the songwriting. Like the *Something New* album, a combination of originals and covers. When they did someone else's songs that was where the Beatles were a real rock 'n' roll band. And they really created the idea of a rock band doing a certain canon of hard-hitting, fast, 'get people up on their feet and dance to' sound.

"In the Beatles," dissects Dr. Cushing, "Paul's bass playing was supportive and creative. Solid and danceable. Always giving an underpinning for the whole song. John Lennon's rhythm guitar playing used to seem buried a bit in the mix on the earlier releases. On the current CD reissues it's up a bit this time around. Instrumentally he served the song. This was a writer's band, not a virtuoso player's band.

Chris Hillman photo by Jim Dickson/Henry Diltz Archives

"The contributions of George Harrison tend to get overlooked a bit. I just read something about just how good were the Beatles? Their third best songwriter was awesome. He was the sanest of them all. The ultimate team player. The one who thought to bring Billy Preston into the *Let It Be* sessions, therefore saving the whole thing. His guitar playing was so economical. Everything was there to serve the song. Like a Motown player. Ringo's drum work served the music perfectly. Beat is the first word in their name, after all."

"The Beatles' arrival in February 1964 was such a healing presence after the horror of the Kennedy assassination. They brought such joy and light to the world, the dark clouds were lifted," instills Chris Hillman, bassist and songwriter for the Byrds and co-founder of the Flying Burrito Brothers.

"We were all emulating the Beatles to some degree at first. The Byrds certainly were. And then, I mean, my God, when I joined the Byrds they were still doing Beatlesque songs that Gene was writing. But then we got into doing other material."

In a 2007 interview I published with Byrds guitarist and songwriter Roger McGuinn, he happily shared thoughts about the Beatles and the relationship the Byrds had with them.

In 1964 McGuinn and his fellow band members watched *A Hard Day's Night* in a Hollywood movie theater, and the direction of their group sound was never the same after viewing that flick.

"Chris Hillman is a very gifted musician," stated McGuinn. "The way he transitioned from mandolin to bass was amazing in a very short time. I don't know if he was completely influenced by McCartney but he had this melodic thing. I guess more from being a lead player. He incorporated a lot of leads into his bass playing.

"On 'Mr. Tambourine Man,' when I recorded my vocal, it wasn't to match the Rickenbacker but to get between John Lennon and Bob Dylan's vocal. I wanted to try and hit that niche there between the two of them.

"With the Byrds we overdubbed with the Rickenbacker, like the lead break on 'Eight Miles High' and 'Turn! Turn! Turn!' They were not done with the band track, we just did a rhythm track and I would go in and do the leads until I got it right.

"I loved *Sgt. Pepper's* and thought it was a brilliant album. We loved everything the Beatles did. They were our heroes. They could do no wrong as far as we were concerned. *Sgt. Pepper's* was just incredible. I may have liked some of their earlier stuff a little better, but I did like the production values of *Sgt. Pepper's* and the fact that it all kind of ran together and had a theme, a story.

**Publicist Billy James and Jim (later Roger) McGuinn
photo by Jim Dickson/Henry Diltz Archives**

"There were brilliant moments on the first trip over to England in 1965. We met the Beatles and the Rolling Stones. We had met the Stones before, but we got to hang out together in England. We met a lot of people and hung out at a lot of parties. McCartney gave me a ride in his Aston Martin at a night at a club, the Scotch and St. James. It was amazing. George and I went over our first guitar licks and talked about them and compared notes. Stuff like that. It was incredible. The audiences then in 1965 were basically little girls. And they were screaming and liking it. But the press ate us up because we were billed as 'America's Answer to the Beatles.' And it was like a football game to them. It was a competitive thing," underlined McGuinn.

"In 1967 when we came back again we did a fan club event at the Chalk Farm Roundhouse that I remember. That was fun. At the end of the tour, the Byrds played a surprise gig at Blaises, which Paul McCartney attended. Derek Taylor was our publicity guy who worked with the Beatles. And we turned the Beatles on to Ravi Shankar."

"Hey, everyone loves the Beatles," marvels musician and actor Bill Mumy. "It's the best music ever made, and it's positive and it's truly magic. They are in a category all their own. It was legitimate magic. Individually, they're all great musicians, writers, and singers and at times amazing and brilliant. Well, I won't say Ringo was ever a brilliant songwriter, but John, Paul and George certainly were," reflects Mumy, a recording artist with 10 solo albums to his credit and a veteran of the *Alfred Hitchcock Presents* TV series.

"But when the four of them were together…onstage or with George Martin producing in Abbey Road Studios…they laid all those songs down and they'll live forever and they're just insanely special. Some things just can't be put into words properly to do them justice. I can't describe why the Beatles are so great. They just are.

"I do have a Beatles story and it drives me nuts. Back when I was on *Lost in Space*, [actress] Angela Cartwright and I were invited to see the Beatles at the Hollywood Bowl. And we were invited to meet them after the gig. OK? OK. Well, I didn't want to go. Let me say that again. I didn't want to go. I remember saying, 'It's just gonna be thousands of people screaming nonstop. I'd rather stay home and listen to the Kingston Trio.' Or something like that.

"I *liked* the Beatles in 1965, but I was a folk music snob and I didn't really get it then. So I passed on seeing the Beatles and meeting them. And Ange has this great picture of her with all four Beatles...and every time I see that picture, I know I could've been right next to her with them. But...I wasn't. And sadly, that's my Beatles story."

**The Beatles at the Hollywood Bowl, August, 1965
courtesy of Harold Sherrick**

Heather Harris, a graduate of the Westlake School For Girls and a music photographer and visual artist, attended the Beatles' 1964 and '65 seismic Hollywood Bowl concerts and their '66 Dodger Stadium show in Los Angeles. She provides a memory of when the band came to play in L.A.

"Teenaged and/or pre-teenaged *recherche du temps perdu* remain notoriously inaccurate, ruled as they are by hormonal, passionate emotions rather than staunch objectivity. However, this former pre-teen well recalls the first Beatles concert at the Hollywood Bowl, oasis of wondrousness observed in an otherwise dire pre-adolescence.

"I was a powerless pre-teen, landlocked in my passions for doing visual art and following music by a familial regime bent on churning out clones of socialite, debutante, non-vocational mommy-track forebears devoid of outside purpose. Listening to my transistor radio under the pillows in bed at night, I heard 'I Want to Hold Your Hand' (the first widespread U.S. Beatles release) and the earth shifted on its axis for me.

"It's said that universal pop music introduces pre-adolescent females to the opposite sex by offering slightly gender-neutral totems of directed passion, not too scary or overtly sexual, from Avalon to Cassidy to Bieber. In the case of the Beatles, this is hogwash. No matter how thoroughly Brian Epstein cleaned them up, the bad boys came through, much as the syndrome had with early Elvis Presley despite his Colonel.

"As with early-'60s European *nouvelle vague* movie stars, the Beatles' outsider long hair signified danger and a new generation's look. The self-written, self-performed, harder rock music also denoted a demographic sea change of non-formulaic, uncontrolled talents, which spilled over into all the arts. And those witty press conferences, with Lennon & Co.'s ad libs, added just the right *frisson* of intellectualism to rope in smart teens. Overall assessment: every young female I knew, from honor students to proto-slackers, wanted to fuck a Beatle. (And some actually did. But that's another tale.) I even made pocket change drawing fellow student/clients *en flagrante* with their favorite Beatle or Rolling Stone.

"However, as a powerless pre-teen, scalper ticket prices were not at my avail, plus the 1964 Hollywood Bowl appearance sold out within hours the same day, an impossible barrier to pre-Internet, non-driving pre-teens. (Los Angeles then as now has no really reliable public transportation.)

"I desperately prevailed upon every entertainment biz contact in my purview, which meant fellow classmates' parents who, however, only directed such efforts towards their own progeny. My own parents were virulently anti-showbiz, since my former singer father had quit with an 'If I can't, nobody in this family can!' obstructionism (to last all my life).

"Last resort: my parents' friends at their church. Where I struck gold. One of their church chums was Randy Wood, president of Dot Records and Ranwood Records (sample artists: Ivory Joe Hunter, Pat Boone, the Del-Vikings, Arthur Alexander, Jimmy Gilmer & the Fireballs—pals of Buddy Holly with a giant hit record 'Sugar Shack'), which had distribution ties to Vee-Jay Records, which, unbeknownst to most all but completionist record collectors, was the Beatles' first record label in America until Capitol Records sorted out their domestic ownership of them via EMI.

"Randy told me to not count on it, and kindly gave me the consolation prize of a Beatles' interview 45 record. This was a promo item with dead air time for whatever DJ at whatever radio station to ask the Beatles questions, then the pre-recorded Beatles provided answers afterwards. This gift engendered a great introduction to the real world of the music business at a tender age!

"Then he came through with a single ticket. Much negotiation to get parents to drop off and pick up. Reward: 35 minutes of audience hysteria and itty bitty Beatles! But no complaints. One could see they did play their own plugged-in instruments, even if one could barely hear same or any vocals whatsoever. In-person vindication! (Answer to unspoken question: even the teens I knew with good cameras and telephoto lenses got terrible pics, given the huge distance betwixt audience and band. With my then crap equipment I didn't even bother.

"I attended the next year's Hollywood Bowl and following year's Dodger Stadium shows as well, the last one with teen musician guy friends who tried to document same on one of the era's giant reel-to-reel tape recorders. I was dragooned into smuggling the enormous interloping machine in my typical girl's beach bag. The straw-woven bag burst under the weight and spilt one reel of tape unspooling down an entire bleacher stairs in the stadium, top to bottom. Tape undamaged, hasty retrenching and re-spooling unseen by the long arms of the law. Of course all my guy friends got was the din of audience screaming…"

Beatles Hollywood Bowl photo courtesy of Harold Sherrick

"Was I a super fan of the Beatles? That would be a major understatement," avows bandleader, Chicano rocker and East Los Angeles music scholar Mark Guerrero. "I don't think there's anyone who could possibly love them more. I've often said that they're the best thing that ever happened to me. The influence they had on me and the pleasure and enjoyment I derived from them and their music is incalculable. I saw their *Ed Sullivan* appearances. I bought 'I Want to Hold Your Hand' when it came out. I also bought *Meet the Beatles!* when it first came out and loved it. I was on board from the beginning. I bought every album when it came out and learned all the songs on them.

Part 2: Last Second of a Big Dream

"My first band, the Escorts, later Mark & the Escorts, started in 1963, before the Beatles emerged in the U.S. There were lots of bands in East L.A. already. Bands in East L.A. were playing R&B, doo-wop, and surf songs. My band started with surf songs, i.e. Dick Dale, the Ventures, and songs like 'Wipe Out' and 'Pipeline.' We also did a little blues, but we started with just instrumentals.

"My band began to sprinkle its repertoire with Beatle songs and continued to do so throughout the '60s, as it evolved into Mark & the Escorts, the Men From S.O.U.N.D., and Nineteen Eighty Four.

"When the Beatles came out Mark & the Escorts started to learn Beatle tunes and do them at our gigs. We did songs like 'I Want to Hold Your Hand,' 'Anna,' 'Twist and Shout,' 'A Hard Day's Night,' 'And I Love Her,' and 'I'll Cry Instead.' The Beatles heard the Eastside Sound. Listen to the clave instrument on their 'And I Love Her.' The Men From S.O.U.N.D. performed 'The Word,' 'Drive My Car' and 'Taxman.'

"Not all East L.A. bands embraced the Beatles. Besides us, I remember some of the others that played Beatles songs were the Emeralds, the Ambertones, the Blendells and Thee Midniters. The ones that didn't were partial to R&B and soul music. Some of those bands later were more likely to play songs by the Rolling Stones or the Kinks.

"My band was part of a music boom in East Los Angeles which happened simultaneously to the Liverpool explosion. Like in Liverpool, East L.A. had countless bands and plenty of venues in which to play.

"In the period of 1964 to '65, East L.A. produced several bands who had national and international hits such as the Premiers ('Farmer John'), the Blendells ('La La La La La'), and Cannibal & the Headhunters ('Land of a Thousand

Dances'). It is at this point that East L.A. met Liverpool for the first time.

"In 1965, Cannibal & the Headhunters' manager, Eddie Davis, got a phone call from Brian Epstein inviting Cannibal & the Headhunters to join the current Beatles tour, which was in progress. They were put on a plane to New York for their first concert with the Beatles, which turned out to be the historic Shea Stadium concert. They went on to play other venues in the tour, including the Houston Astrodome and the Hollywood Bowl.

"I was fortunate to personally witness the Hollywood Bowl concert, where Cannibal & the Headhunters made a good accounting of themselves and got the best response of any of the opening acts. They were a dancing vocal group like the Temptations. We played with Cannibal & the Headhunters.

"I also saw the Beatles at Balboa Stadium in San Diego in 1965 and Dodger Stadium in 1966," proudly expresses Guerrero, who holds a B.A. degree in Chicano Studies from Cal State University Los Angeles.

"Anyway, I could go on and on about the Beatles. To this day I can't get enough of reading about them, seeing documentaries, finding bootleg stuff and outtakes, etc. They still inspire me.

"I've been to Liverpool twice, in 2004 and 2006, and played the Cavern. I was also on BBC Merseyside radio on both trips doing interviews. I met and played with many of the musicians who shared the bill with the Beatles at the Cavern and in Hamburg, such as Kingsize Taylor & the Dominoes, guys from the Undertakers, Faron of Faron's Flamingos, and many others.

"I visited all the Beatle sites such as Strawberry Field, Penny Lane, the church in Woolton where John and Paul first met, their childhood homes, John Lennon's high school and grammar school, etc. I've written articles on my trips with photo galleries, sound bites, and the radio shows at these links on my website:

www.markguerrero.com/32.php
www.markguerrero.com/47.php.

"The former article is titled *East L.A. Meets Liverpool.* Those trips, which I did alone, were two of the best experiences of my life."

Guerrero, son of the legendary bandleader and composer Lalo Guerrero, the father of Chicano music, was also part of *American Sabor: Latinos in U.S. Popular Music,* a free bilingual exhibit and series of programs developed by the Experience Music Project Museum and the University of Washington and organized by the Smithsonian Institution Travelling Exhibition Services, that spotlighted the influence of Latino music; it was featured on the campus of CSULA from December 2, 2013, to February 9, 2014.

Prominently on display was a photograph of Frankie Garcia, the lead vocalist of Cannibal & the Headhunters, with Paul McCartney.

"We liked the Beatles from the time Billy Preston came back from Europe and knew about them," raves Johnny Echols, guitarist and co-founder of Love. "I had played with Billy before Love, and he was a good friend, and I met them in 1965. They sent us backstage passes for the Hollywood Bowl show. I went with a fantastic jazz musician, Michael Bolivar.

"It was loud. And we saw this fantastic thing that we had not expected. At that time there was this thing happening with the audience and the musician but never like this. I mean, this was over the top. And that was the point and I had to tell Arthur [Lee] about it. 'This is where we want to go, man.' We wanted to leave the chitlin' circuit and whatever that's gonna be behind. And we want to move to this circuit. 'Cause this is where the money's at and this is where all the happenings are. 'Cause they can play the kind of music they want, out of respect, be revered, loved and have this huge audience.' That was where we wanted to go. Absolutely."

"My aunt Maggie bought me my first record, *Meet the Beatles!*, in 1964 when I was 11 years old at the Kress store in downtown L.A. -- and I was hooked for life," conceded Gene Aguilera, East L.A. music historian, USC graduate, and author of *Mexican American Boxing in Los Angeles* (Arcadia Publishing).

"Every Friday night, my Grandmother 'Mama' Carmen and I would catch the No. 47 bus line by our apartment in Boyle Heights and take off for the big city to meet my aunt as soon as she got off work as a seamstress. We'd walk around a bit, duck into Clifton's for dinner, then go shopping at Kress, and there it was—the record section! You know, this was right after the Beatles appeared on *The Ed Sullivan Show* and excitement was high. Ah...1964, it was a very good year.

"I remember in grammar school, kids would ask, 'Beatles or Beach Boys?' and I always would choose the lads from Liverpool, because their sound, hair, and clothes was so different than anything else. Even though I love surf music, those 'high-waters' pants the Beach Boys wore would get you thrown out of East L.A.

"The Beatles put their thumbprint on East L.A. music, all right. Influential East L.A. band Thee Midniters recorded two Beatle cover songs ('Slow Down' and 'Money') on their first LP, cut 'Yesterday' on their third LP Unlimited, and on the holy grail series of East L.A. collectible records, *The Salesian High School Rock 'n' Roll Show Volume 2*, they waxed 'And

I Love Her.' Cesar Rosas of Los Lobos showed me on guitar how 'This Boy' was written with East L.A. chord changes that could be heard on a million oldie songs.

"Listening to KRLA on my tiny transistor radio, I heard the announcement that the Beatles were coming to Dodger Stadium! They were going to perform at the same place where Sandy Koufax was leading our beloved Dodgers to the World Series," continued Gene. "I pleaded with my aunt Julie to take me to buy tickets, and luckily we got in to see them for $6 a pop on Sunday evening, August 28, 1966. Opening acts Bobby Hebb ('Sunny'), the Cyrkle ('Turn-Down Day') and the Ronettes ('Be My Baby'), perhaps without Ronnie Spector, prepared us for a 30-minute hit-filled, packed set by the Beatles, who were onstage at second base.

Dodger Stadium ticket from KRLA Presents The Beatles courtesy of Harvey Kubernik

"As soon as it was over they ducked into a tent behind the stage and roared off in a speeding car as guards quickly opened the center field wall. Just like that, they were gone before we even left our seats.

"Every once in a while I pull out *Meet the Beatles!* and spin it on my turntable. It takes me back to 1964 when I first saw them on the *Sullivan* show. Trust me, I will never sell this copy and feel comforted by the fact that I will pass it on to my daughters who can play it and visit 1964 anytime they want to."

> "Let's say that the last rock and roll show you caught was one of the historic Beatles shows, back in '64/'65. It was planting your anatomy on a slab of concrete in a jam-packed football stadium, enduring the half dozen or so less-than-spectacular supporting acts while waiting anxiously the appearance of the Liverpool four.
>
> "And when they appeared—mop-topped and uniformly dressed—the jet engine-sized screams of the mob virtually obliterated their musical output. Oh, for a rousing finale, a platoon of cops scrimmaged a surprisingly resilient squad of young, female Beatlemaniacs, down around the forty yard line."
>
> –John Gilliland, Chapter 20: *Sgt. Pepper at the Summit, The Pop Chronicles*, 1969, on KRLA 1110 AM radio.

"I saw the Beatles in Portland, Maine," Allen Ginsberg told me in a 1995 interview. "I was up there with Gary Snyder, probably 1965, 1966. In my *Collected Poems* it's dated by a poem describing the Beatles playing in Portland. I was with a couple of little children. I had gotten tickets and was sitting way out in the bleachers, and John Lennon came out and said, 'We understand that Allen Ginsberg is in the audience. So three cheers! So now we'll have our show.' He saluted me from the stage, which amazed me and made me feel very proud with all these young kids at my side," beamed Allen, who was in the documentary *It Was 20 Years Ago Today* that focused on *Sgt. Pepper's Lonely Hearts Club Band*.

"In the late '60s or early '70s I visited McCartney in London. I was on TV that day, a pro-pot rally in Hyde Park, and the cops had stopped me from playing a harmonium or talking on a microphone. So I came down from my ladder from where I was talking and gave the cop a flower. That was kind of a knockout for everybody in London at that time, rather than getting mad. And I was watching that on TV with Mick Jagger at McCartney's house. And McCartney was painting a satin shirt and he gave it to me as a performance shirt."

In March 1975, the Robert Stigwood office requested me to attend the *Tommy* movie premiere, their film adaptation of the Who's rock opera, at the Fox Wilshire. At the reception in the lobby following the screening, I was seated with Paul and Linda McCartney. Delightful couple. In 1975 I interviewed Paul for the Japanese periodical *Music Life*.

When Allen died in 1997, I mailed McCartney my Allen Ginsberg tribute cover story interview in *The Los Angeles Times* Calendar section that contained a picture of Paul and Allen during their poetry and music performance in England held at the Royal Albert Hall.

In 1999, Paul McCartney and Capitol Records were hosting a listening party in West Hollywood at the House of Blues for his just issued *Run Devil Run*.

I was given a full access laminate for the pre-show bash. I was standing in the Foundation Room with Brian Wilson, Phil Everly, Gwen Stefani, Rodney Bingenheimer and Tony Fonaro. Paul noticed Rodney and waived us all over to his area. "I've known Rodney a long time." They had hung out together years earlier at a Peggy Lee recording session Paul produced on Peggy at the Record Plant studio. In the mid-nineties Rodney attended a Linda and Paul McCartney photo book reception on La Brea Avenue.

I reminded Paul I had conducted a couple of extensive interviews in 1996 with Allen Ginsberg around his recent "The Ballad of the Skeletons" recording where he overdubbed some instruments on the track. Paul said Ginsberg visited his family home in England and he did some 8mm filming of him.

In 2003, McCartney's office called and invited me to a cast-and-crew screening of his *Back in the U.S.* concert film in Hollywood. In the lobby Paul mentioned Ginsberg. "Allen was a lovely man."

In 2004 I was preparing one Ginsberg interview to be published in my debut book, *This Is Rebel Music*. Subsequently, a month later, Paul arranged for a photo of himself and Allen together, taken by Linda McCartney, at that Royal Albert Hall poetry and music event, to be sent for inclusion in my book.

Right after *This Is Rebel Music* was published I mailed a copy to Paul's office in the U.K. His daughter Mary McCartney took the portrait photograph of Marianne Faithfull, who is profiled in the pages as well.

Last decade I was in a Studio City health food restaurant one afternoon with Nancy Rose Retchin. It was just an hour after I introduced her to my neighbor, the artist and photographer Heather Harris. Both were veterans of the 1966 Beatle concert at Dodger Stadium. Nancy gifted me her ticket stub from that show.

During our meal, Nancy suddenly uttered the words, "Harvey, Paul McCartney is walking towards our table."

"Hey mate." We talked for 10 minutes.

I think Paul was sort of impressed when I immediately wanted to know about his tune and musical arrangement for Cilla Black's "Step Inside Love," which George Martin produced. "Been a while since anyone asked about that Cil record," he smiled.

Paul and I talked about a couple of authors we both knew and then he wanted to know if I was working on another book. I said yes—a rock 'n' roll soundtrack and film examination, *Hollywood Shack Job*. I told him that Andrew Loog Oldham had just cited his "Live and Let Die" James

Bond theme in an email interview with me just the week before: "It was very clever and Paul did his homework. He had this and that to remind him of earlier things with Bond. He had the tonal space."

McCartney grinned when he further learned that I had just captioned a 1989 Henry Diltz photo of him in the morning sitting at a piano inside one of the Capitol Records studio rooms. Nancy and I were actually on our way back to Henry's photography studio after our late lunch.

As Andrew Loog Oldham has demonstrated to me more than a few times, "there are no coincidences."

"I was a good friend of Linda Eastman before she married Paul," volunteered Diltz. "We were fellow photographers. I initially met her in New York at a photo lab. In very early 1971 Linda called me on the telephone and asked that I come see her and Paul in Malibu, where they were renting a house. They needed some photos taken for the *Ram* songbook. I brought some joints and we smoked them. We sat around the pool and Paul was strumming his ukulele and I kept photographing them. We had lunch. I photographed that. They needed a nice portrait of the two of them, and we went and found a nice little place where they could crouch down with some flowers behind them.

"Then Linda said, 'We want to see these pictures first thing in the morning because we want to pick one out for the cover of *LIFE* magazine.'

"So I went back the next morning with the developed film slides and they picked out one shot and it was flown to New York. It was an article on Paul, but they were originally gonna use a Beatle picture. And I shot Paul and Linda in color, but the magazine had to print it in black-and-white because there wasn't time to print it in color. And it wasn't nearly as good.

**Paul and Linda McCartney, Malibu, 1971
photo by Henry Diltz**

"When the graphic artist Gary Burden was laying out the *RAM* songbook with my pictures he asked me if I would letter, hand print the songs. So I did kind of an art deco printing.

"I later did photos for Wings' *London Town* sessions that became a poster inside. I spent a week with them in the Virgin Islands on a boat."

Part 2: Last Second of a Big Dream

**Paul Mc Cartney, Virgin Islands, May 1977
photo by Henry Diltz**

It Was 50 Years Ago Today: The Beatles Invade America and Hollywood

PART 3: PRICK UP YOUR EARS

The late musician and songwriter Doug Fieger was chief member of the Knack, who were best known for their No. 1 smash "My Sharona," on the Capitol label.

Years ago I talked to Doug about the Beatles. Fieger owned some really fab vintage gear.

"The Beatles were unique. They had a unique harmonic structure. It was joyous. And it was good," he said.

"They did whatever was necessary because of the limited amount of tracks. And they always, almost, had all four of them playing at once. So they were performances of each part of the song. So it wasn't just tracking and overdubbing. Because of the way they had to record. So all four of them would get an assignment. A shaker, a maraca or percussion track.

"George Martin brought humor because he was a comedy producer. He did the *Goon Show* record. He kept it clever and he also brought a musicality and an arrangement sense that they then learned from, obviously. But at the very beginning it was him.

"I think more importantly than sonically, all the studios at the time were treated fairly similarly. That the plainness of the working space contributed much more than the sound.

"If you record a sound well and then you treat it then you have good microphones. EMI made their own custom boards for all the Abbey Road studios in places like India and in Nigeria. The only place that didn't get them was Capitol

Records in the U.S. The record label we were on," said the proud 12-string Rickenbacker owner.

"They made me want to be a songwriter," said Doug. "I never even considered that. I was an actor when I was a young kid before the Beatles came along. I was more inclined to be a personality or a DJ than a songwriter or performer. The whole English invasion and the pop explosion in the early and mid-60s.

"The Beatles make me smile. It's an intangible. In the same way Brian Wilson's song do. It touches a place in your youth that you remember but it's much, much deeper than that. Its kid's music but it's not for kids.

"The Beatles have a canon of 150 songs and every single one of them is a hit. Even the ones they didn't write. You just can't beat that. I recorded in Abbey Road. With the Knack we recorded 'My Sharona' there to play the backing track for *Tops Of The Pops*. We did a live vocal on TV. I was smiling so hard I can't express to you what it was like being there. The joy.

"I didn't hear the Motown songs through the Beatles. I was in Detroit and age 11 when I first heard the Beatles. It resonated better. I really have to say. Their version of 'Money (That's What I Want)' is deranged. Down to the atonal piano hits. It's Lennon at his most primitive," construes Doug.

"I love the versions by the Marvelettes and the Miracles. But the Beatles had those voices. They used to plug straight into the wall. They didn't use amplifiers. Everything was being done 'make it up as you go along and make hits.'

"And the biggest part of that were songs. 'The play is the thing.' Songs and the song is the thing. You cannot make up for a great song with production or recording. Record producer Jimmy Miller used to tell me, 'You put a great band with a great song in a studio and with one microphone in the middle of the room I can make a hit.'

"'How do you get a Beatles sound?' People ask me all the time," shrugged Fieger. "Earlier in the decade we encored with 'A Hard Day's Night.' Well I say, for the early Beatles sound, you get flat wound strings and their fingers. That's how you get a Beatles sound.

"'In My Life' is my favorite Beatles song. It's a great song. It's an incredibly perfectly written song. The production on 'Hello Goodbye' is as good as any production I've ever heard.

"The best sounding reproductions of the Beatles were 8-track tapes because they were quarter inch tape and it sounds the best. It compresses the sound so it sounds really good on the radio. The Beatles going to digital I notice a difference between the 16 bit masters and the 24 bit masters. Now that you've got high sampling rates it's virtually impossible to start with an analog source to discern the difference. It's stunning and astonishing to hear those records that were recorded 45 years ago.

"I had all the mono records. That is what it is made for. The Beatles would record, hang for the mono mix. And the Beatles were there every day for the mixing of *Sgt. Pepper* and they knew how important it was. It took them months. When they were finished with the mono mix of *Sgt. Pepper*, George Martin and Geoff Emerick were entrusted to produce the stereo version in four days. And the stereo version is the only version we've been able to get for how many years? And I believe it's just as great as the mono.

"How do I describe the mono mix of *Sgt. Pepper*? It's telescopic. It's not spread. So each different sound is placed in the mono field coming at you. And it's a whole other experience.

"Mono is different. Like on their *White* Album. 'Long Long Long,' 'Revolution 9,' and 'Helter Skelter' are completely different recordings.

"Jack Douglas, who produced the Knack's third album told me a story that Lennon was at a party one time. And he hadn't heard the Beatles' records in a long time. He was sitting in front of the stereo, put on a Beatles record and he was sitting there and then this look came over his face and he moved over to the left speaker. Then he moved over to the right speaker and he was flabbergasted. There were only vocals coming out of the left speaker. And only backing tracks on the right speaker. And he had never heard that before ever. And he went out the next day and bought all of the albums by the Beatles on Capitol Records because he had never heard them done like that.

"The Beatles are not a band." Fieger pleaded. "Dare I say avatars. They came to this earth with powers and abilities far beyond mortal man. *[Laughs.]* And the four of them did. There was an energy.

"Ringo went to one of my weddings. The St. James Club on Sunset. Him and his wife."

The night before Doug died, Ringo Starr visited him, and while he was sleeping, Ringo quietly sang "She Loves You" to him at his bedside.

Gary Pig Gold started up Canada's very first music fanzine, *The Pig Paper*. Gary's widely syndicated "Pigshit" column recently entered its third decade of regular publication. Gold further praises the joys of the Beatles in mono:

"As I believe Doug Fieger already stated, the (pre-'68) Beatles in mono WAS the State of the Art!! Like all Sixties Top 40–bound pop, it was arranged and mixed to play back most powerfully through a single, six-transistor radio speaker. But even *Pepper* sounds best monophonically. And don't just take it from Beatlegeeks like us, either: To quote Abbey Road tape operator Richard Lush (from Mark Lewisohn's landmark *The Complete Beatles Recording Sessions* book),

'The only real version of *SPLHCB* is the mono version. The Beatles were there for all the mono mixes. Then, after the album was finished George Martin, Geoff Emerick and I did the stereo in a few days, just the three of us, without a Beatle in sight. There are all sorts of things on the mono, little effects here and there, which the stereo doesn't have.'"

Record producer and guitarist David Kessel, who heads the www.cavehollywood.com website recorded with John Lennon on the Phil Spector-produced *Rock 'n' Roll* album in 1973 at the Record Plant in Los Angeles. In a 2012 phone interview, Kessel provided insights about finding and hearing the Beatles in mono.

"It's the way Americans heard the original records. As for mono, well, first of all, it's all powerful and coming out of both speakers the same. OK? That means you are getting the full signal right at you. Like with Phil Spector's 'Wall of Sound' in mono, you are now having to worry about stereo placement. OK?

"Originally, you were or are making these records for a transistor radio. And ultimately you want it to sound really great out of that small transistor radio speaker. You're also thinking in terms of when the needle goes down on the record. It's going to go out through the needle as a whole signal. Whereas when you start dividing the instruments, 'part of this on the left side, part of this on the right side,' you can hear that on that on some of the Beatles' mid- career records, trying to get a stereo thing going, but you lose the full impact of the solid centered power. With mono you get a thicker piece of music on tape."

"As a teen growing up in America, music excited me more than hot rods, sports, or even girls," affirms Alex Del Zoppo, keyboardist and co-founder of the seminal band Sweetwater, who performed at the 1969 Woodstock music festival.

"Early R&B and rock held my attention as I grew from a 'party musician' into a 'working musician' while still in junior high through high school. I learned every variation of blues and rock pattern possible, and was just beginning to become somewhat bored with playing the same stuff over and over at gig after gig.

"Then the Beatles came. At first, they seemed lukewarm when they covered American hit songs, and their original songs, though played with a certain amount of enthusiasm, had bubblegum lyric themes. Consequently, I dismissed them as only a cultural phenomenon, given their looks, etc. But they soon got my attention...in a positive way: through the rapid progress of their original music. They began to use melodies that painted outside of the lines we had all grown so used to, and to use chords that were unexpected surprises, pulling our emotions in directions that were totally new to us. Their lyrics began to grow up, too—covering subjects that had serious social implications. More important," Alex says, "they continually grew with each new record, and did this as the entire world was paying attention. And because of that timing, they single-handedly advanced popular music to the endless spectrum it is now—all within just a few years, opening up possibilities to everyone who heard them, including other musicians, songwriters and performers. Because their personal evolution changed everything, I will always view popular music as either 'Before Beatles' or 'Post-Beatles.' And I feel extremely fortunate to have experienced it all. What a ride," acknowledges the Los Angeles native.

Dr. Timothy Leary, one of the voices on John Lennon and Yoko Ono's "Give Peace a Chance," might have agreed with Doug Fieger. Leary once portrayed the Beatles in a media appearance thusly: "I declare that the Beatles are mutants. Prototypes of evolutionary agents sent by God, endowed with a mysterious power to create a new human species, a young race of laughing freemen."

In 1996 I was blessed to have a meeting and then a music-oriented interview with teacher and philosopher Ram Dass, the author of *Be Here Now*. Of course I posed a question about the Beatles.

"I loved the Beatles' music. I took acid to *Sgt. Pepper.* What I loved was that these experiences were community and ritual of a very high order, where people felt safe to be open and very uninhibited, and there was a sweetness about it all. Music is a vehicle for moving consciousness, and humor is a vehicle for moving consciousness. And the combination of that.

"It was not hard rock. It was soft rock. It was John Lennon's love. It was that quality of that space. I listened to FM radio and everyone around me had the albums. I met John Lennon and Yoko Ono. They came to my apartment in New York to meet me and [director] Peter Brook. John was very sweet and available and very curious and thoughtful. I found him a very loving being to be with."

Deepak Chopra, M.D., is chief executive officer of the Chopra Center for Wellbeing in La Jolla, California. He is a best-selling author whose many works include *The Seven Spiritual Laws of Success* and *The Path to Love*. He was formerly chief of staff at New England Memorial Hospital, and also taught at Tufts University and Boston University

School of Medicine. He is recognized for his role in bringing time-honored Eastern principles to the Western world. In 1998 I interviewed him at the Sunset Marquis Hotel in West Hollywood.

"In the '60s I was a fan of the Beatles. I bought *Sgt. Pepper's* in India. I heard a lot of music on the BBC in India, and was brought up on classical sounds, Mozart, Vivaldi, Beethoven. Indian classical music, Ravi Shankar, Ali Akbar Khan. And the Beatles.

"*Sgt. Pepper's* was the right thing at the right time. It was an interesting time. When people were kind of playing with drugs a little bit, the hallucinogenics, and causing some drastic mind shifts in people. I was in medical school at the time *Sgt. Pepper's* came out. A friend of mine actually had gone on a scholarship to England and brought back two copies of *Sgt. Pepper's*, one for me and one for himself. And shortly after that, the Beatles arrived in Rishikesh, India, in 1968.

"I grew up watching Ravi Shankar. Teenage years. I didn't meet George until 20 years later. Actually, I was introduced to Ravi through George. It's interesting that George introduced me to a fellow Indian."

Jazz musicians, session players, and Hollywood studio arrangers were not immune to the repertoire of the Beatles.

A trend turned homage might have begun in spring 1964 with Stu Phillips and the Hollyridge Strings creating an instrumental *Beatles Songbook* LP, followed by Jack Nitzsche and His Orchestra recording *Dance to the Hits of the Beatles.*

Bud Shank had a MOR hit with "Michelle"; the Paul Horn Quintet covered "Norwegian Wood." *Rubber Soul Jazz* was produced by Marshall Lieb and arranged by Wrecking Crew architect Don Randi, while the Randi Trio did *Revolver*

Jazz. Shank would later cut an entire LP titled *Magical Mystery*, arranged and conducted by Bob Florence.

A popular KMET-FM staple in Hollywood was Gary Burton's own meditative rendition of "Norwegian Wood." AM radio outlet KMPC was partial to Count Basie and His Orchestra's *Basie's Beatle Bag* platter.

Gábor Szabó also incorporated several Beatles tunes on his *1969* album for Gary McFarland's Skye label, which was located in Southern California.

The KUSC-FM radio station at the University of Southern California on their *Underground Airbag* program added at one time on their coveted playlist, the late, great English jazz pianist Gordon Beck, who in 1967 released the epochal *Experiments in Pop*, housing a radically jazzed-up version of "Norwegian Wood (The Bird Has Flown)," featuring the up-and-coming guitarist John McLaughlin.

In 1966, saxophonist Charles Lloyd, who earned a degree in music from USC, formed the Charles Lloyd Quartet. In 1967, the group, pianist Keith Jarrett, bassist Ron McClure and drummer Jack DeJohnette, recorded Lloyd's *Love-In* at San Francisco's Fillmore Auditorium which contained "Here There and Everywhere." KBRU-FM the student-run operation at UCLA had five copies in their library!

Pasadena's KPPC-FM in 1971 also tracked the power duo of drummer Pete York, formerly of Spencer Davis and organist Eddie Hardin, who cut a "Prog" version of "Norwegian Wood," that is considered a cult classic.

But at the short-lived club, The Chez, on Santa Monica Boulevard (formerly The Action), the newly-minted Buddy Rich Big Band turned "Norwegian Wood" into a roiling brass-and-reed flagwaver in 1966.

The band did turn-away business at the Hollywood club, and Dick Bock captured the electricity on the best-selling *Big*

Swing Face album for World Pacific. Arranger Bill Holman's chart on "Norwegian Wood" was an instant crowd pleaser, as it is this day when it's played at the L.A. Jazz Institute's biannual big band jazz weekends.

One of the best Beatles jazz interpretations was on the Pacific Jazz label. "Eleanor Rigby," heard on *Live at the Lighthouse '68* by the Jazz Crusaders.

In the Los Angeles market for many years, radio station KBCA-FM spun Ramsey Lewis Trio's swinging *A Hard Day's Night* live at the Lighthouse venue. "And I Love Her" is in the same set.

"The hip jazz crowd clearly recognizes the tunes and sings along on that disc. I guess Beatles songs just sound better by the Pacific Ocean," suggests KCPR-FM DJ, Dr. James Cushing, who for the last 30 years has hosted a Coastal California-based jazz show. "Or is it just that proximity to any large body of water gives Liverpool-grown music a context that fits?

"Steve Marcus & Larry Coryell did lengthy, crazy-ass free jazz and distorted guitar versions of 'Rain' and 'Tomorrow Never Knows.'

"Stanley Turrentine and his organ-playing wife Shirley Scott coaxed the grease out of 'Can't Buy Me Love' live at The Front Room in Newark NJ in 1964. Impulse Records released it. Grant Green titled one of his albums *I Want to Hold Your Hand*. Frank Sinatra sang 'Something' on the *Trilogy* triple-LP. Freddie Hubbard did a wicked cover of 'Cold Turkey' during the Red Clay sessions in New York City.

"This is the way songs survive -- by being reinterpreted again and again. Beatles songs adapt themselves well to jazz because they contain the essential mystery of art; they remain exactly what they are no matter the style in which they're presented. The same is true of Cole Porter, the Gershwins, Rodgers/Hart, and Johnny Mercer."

Well into the late Seventies, the Jazz great, veteran studio musician, and former (1956-1960) Verve Records A&R man, guitarist Barney Kessel, on occasion would eventually insert "Yesterday" in his live solo bookings.

And, decades ago, musician and Chapman Stick instrument inventor Emmett Chapman with Knack drummer Bruce Gary inserted "Fool on the Hill" from *Magical Mystery Tour* to their memorable Kerckhoff Coffee House duo evenings on the campus of UCLA.

John Van Hamersveld's commercial artistic journey began with the *Endless Summer* poster. What followed were more than 300 album covers, including designs for the Beatles' American pressing of *Magical Mystery Tour*, Jefferson Airplane's *Crown of Creation*, and the Beach Boys' *Wild Honey*, while he headed the art department at Capitol Records from 1965 to 1968 inside the Tower building in Hollywood.

"I started with the *Endless Summer* poster in 1963 as a graphic design student, later being reconstructed for a Sandals soundtrack for Bruce Brown's *The Endless Summer* movie album created by World Pacific in1966.

"I was recommended by my instructor friend and Ed Ruscha at a lunch one day, who suggested I could call Capitol Records and meet a director in art services," Van Hamersveld remembered. "I was 25 years old and without a job. I had an art school portfolio from Chouinard Art Institute/Cal Arts, there was some *Surfer* magazines from the early jobs at *Surfer* and the new Day-Glo *Endless Summer* poster.

"I made the call to the Capitol art department, and they answered and gave me an appointment. Later, I went for an interview at Capitol Records and showed the poster to George Osaki of creative services at the Capitol Records building, on the sixth floor, in 1967. He recommended me to Brown Meggs, who was the vice president of the CRDC, the Capitol Records Distribution Company."

John further detailed the backstory to his relationship with Brown Meggs. "The first meeting at the circular Capitol building that looked like a stack of records was with George Osaki's. I chatted and showed my work of commercial images I had done for other corporations.

"I had rented the Coronado Studio near Otis Art Institute where my girlfriend was a student. George, as the director of the art services, then asked me to report to the eighth floor of the Capitol Records building on Vine Street. As I stepped off the eighth floor from the elevator I then turned left and walked into the office of Brown Meggs," Van Hamersveld recollected.

"He appeared in front of me and addressed me quickly, saying, 'You are going to take this job and you can't turn the job down.' I paused for the moment. Here I was in the air-conditioning of the executive offices. It was a new status for me to do work here and get paid.

"We're in his office face to face, door is closed behind me. Brown tells me of Brian Epstein's suicide. He managed the Beatles. Brown reaches over to desk for a small EP album cover, and shows the cover to me and says, this is the Beatles new album we received from EMI. He says, 'How can I sell this to the stores? I am the vice president of the CRDC. What do I do with this? John, you are my art director!' We begin to sit down. As I am thinking on my feet at this point, he sits down in his chair in the executive small room. He says, 'The news on this *Magical Mystery Tour* video movie for the BBC is a flop! What do you think you can do to put this together with the tune titles to sell it to the consumer?' I say, 'OK, I'll take it home tonight and figure it out!' So I am sent home to do the work at my studio as a private contractor, separated from Capitol Records staff, or art department, where my day-job office is. I sit there in my studio the first night wondering how to solve the problem.

"So, from Brown's point of view, I was to bring the underground graphic look to the EP that EMI had provided," announced Van Hamersveld. "The EP was customed and masked faces of the Beatles. The company had made all their sales on the Beatle portraits on the cover of their albums. This time they didn't have a picture. So I created a graphic style that would complement the photograph. I was the graphic designer and made judgment of what would help sell the drama of the package.

"*Magical Mystery Tour* video movie on the BBC with magic bus idea was a flop. But the album soundtrack was their product to sell to the consumer, packaged in a style to fit the times in the marketplace. On another desk was the Pinnacle poster being made, and both were published at the same time for the same market," specified Van Hamersveld.

"The white walls to the Coronado Studio define the room with two tables to work on. One table has the production work to the first Pinnacle Shrine Exposition poster to be finished to print in AD Print. I wander around for a few minutes and all of it comes to mind. I am thinking, I will flow the EP photo in the larger 12x12 square. I will get a funky font for the tune titles that is in contrast with EP typography. So I get out a pen from a drawer, pull out a piece of paper and draw the background of clouds in black-and-white. I am still up later into the night to finish the drawing. The next day I send the drawing out for a photostat at AD Stat. The stat comes back to the Capitol office. I pick it up and go back to the studio, and on the way across from my studio was the art store, where I buy some Zipatone screen in large dots. So with the type and the supplies to walk into the studio to finish the highly political *Magical Mystery Tour* American cover.

"The single black-and-white drawing and the black dots are layers, with the phototype in an arc, photographically manipulation of the special optical camera-like machine. The position stat of the EP photograph is centered on the production board. This work is called a mechanical as a paste-up on a board. I call out the colors I want in process four-color.

"The magic in this project is understanding the stripping of negatives and exposing them to make a comprehensive color key of the actual production instruction for printing," Van Hamersveld revealed. "About 48 hours has passed as I ready to present the finished color key for Brown to see. The delivery to my office at Capitol arrives in a package from AD Stat. I pick it up and go up the elevator to Brown's office. He greets me kind of sober as I open the package to show the contents. He's excited with a big smile and says, 'You saved it!'

"I call the printer and not show it to them, just print it, put the vinyl in it and show it to the distribution. I left the office. Later I got my check in my girlfriend Honeya's name. Cash it! But never got a published credit.

"I was paid by Capitol off their books as a vendor. That was my night job to pay for my Coronado Studio, there where Pinnacle Dance Concerts was created with my psychedelic poster line, distributed by Personality Poster in New York. My *Endless Summer* poster was hot, and mostly sold out and reordered. After the Beatles' *Magical Mystery Tour* was released I left the company on a leave of absence. Brown was befuddled that I had other things to do."

"1977 saw not one, but *two* new, sort of, Beatles albums in the shops," recalls Gary Pig Gold. "No, not the fabled off-the-Twickenham-floor oldies collection from the 'Get Back'/'Let It Be' sessions—we're *still* waiting for that one!—but somethings equally vintage…and absolutely live.

"One of these items offered a deliciously rough hour or so of the lads ushering in New Year's '63 at what is perhaps their final gig as a bar band, back on their old German stompin' grounds. It's every bit as lo-fi as it is low-down, of course; but where else can you hear John Lennon picking on his nose (as opposed to begging upon knees) during 'Mr. Moonlight,' not to mention changing each of those m's to t's throughout 'Shimmy Shimmy'?

"Hot on the heels of *Live at the Star Club 1962* came the decidedly more cinematic and Technicolor *Beatles at the Hollywood Bowl*, wherein George Martin and his trusty right-hand ears Geoff Emerick took Capitol's original 3-track (!) recordings of our heroes' 1964 and 1965 Bowl shows, as produced on-site by veteran Sinatra/Dino/Garland/Kingston Trio/Dick Dale A&R wiz Voyle Gilmore, spliced, diced, filtered and EQ'd the entire ab-fab cacophony, and produced one state-of-the-mid-Seventies-art composite of both shows onto two crisp, vinyl sides. The packaging was gorgeous, the audio restoration nothing short of impressive, and needless to say, the performances themselves were, and remain, incendiary.

"Plus you even got Sir George M. making a snide remark about the Bay City Rollers on the LP's back cover, just to put things into their proper hysterical '77 perspective. Why the powers-that-are at Apple Corps haven't allowed a reissue of this utterly historic gem yet is beyond you or me."

George Harrison and Rodney Bingenheimer
photo by Ed Caraeff

My Day with George Harrison
By Rodney Bingenheimer

"I first met George and the Beatles after their 1966 concert in L.A. at Dodger Stadium, where I watched it from the dugout with Carl Wilson of the Beach Boys.

"In 1967, George was studying the sitar with Ravi Shankar, his teacher. George was devoting all his time to Indian music. I was writing a weekly music column for *GO* magazine and I was invited to the Kinnara School of Music on Robertson Boulevard, who held a special press conference in honor of Ravi Shankar. George introduced Ravi and also made some comments.

Photographer Ed Caraeff and I witnessed Ravi at the Monterey International Pop Festival the previous June.

"After the conference, George and I talked, and he asked me, 'Do you know where I can get some groovy things?' I sure did, and the next day we went shopping to all sorts of groovy stores in the Hollywood area.

"We went in a '64 copper brown Corvair driven by a secretary from Apple's Derek Taylor. George in the front seat and myself with photographer Ed Caraeff in the back.

"We then drove to a psychedelic head shop in Westwood called Headquarters which Jerry Hopkins owned. George really dug it and flipped out in the black light room. He bought a psychedelic poster of the Beatles and lots of black light posters.

"Then we went to Fred Segal's clothing store on Santa Monica Boulevard at Crescent Heights—before the place moved to Melrose Avenue. George liked everything there and must have purchased $200 of items when we walked out of the door. He bought paisley pants, sunglasses. I got him the heart-shaped-lenses glasses that he eventually wore the next day when he and Pattie Boyd visited San Francisco.

The glasses were built from bicycle reflectors, and when you peeked through them they had little bits of all sorts of colors all mixed up, like a kaleidoscope. Ed took a photo of George and I at the coffee shop on the corner next to Fred Segal's and across the street from the club P.J.'s that became the Starwood.

"We all went to eat at the Broiler Heaven. George didn't eat meat because of his religion so he ordered a cheese sandwich. They served potato salad along with the sandwich, and he didn't know what to do with it—he'd never eaten potato salad before either! He piled it on top of his sandwich and devoured it that way. Then he asked about a chocolate malt and decided to order one.

"George made an effort to play the jukebox on the premises but had some difficulty. He wanted to hear the Doors' 'Light My Fire' and Eric Burdon & the New Animals' 'San Franciscan Nights,' and I then assisted him how to operate the jukebox.

"This was like the first time George was in the United States but not as a member of the Beatles. In 1963 he went to St. Louis to visit his sister Louise before the Beatles first came to America.

"After we ate we did more shopping and drove down Santa Monica Boulevard in the two-door Corvair with a Monterey International Pop Festival sticker on the bumper.

"People recognized him but he didn't get mobbed. He kept saying over and over again how great the people were because they realized that he wanted a little time to be just a normal person and do normal things. Whenever someone did come up, they were very polite, but most of the time when people recognized him they just waved or smiled just to say hi, and carried on about their business. George kept saying that he was going to tell Paul, John and Ringo to come to Hollywood because they could really have a good time here.

"Ed Caraeff had previously discovered an Indian shop also on Santa Monica Boulevard called Sat Parush while eating at an Indonesian restaurant on that block. So George suggested we walk over to Sat Parush. It was the first chance he'd gotten in all these years to just walk on an American street. People were great. They just smiled and waved and nobody tried to mob him. George really liked everyone because they were so nice to him. Ed would later do a photo shoot in 1968 Sat Parush of a Strawberry Alarm Clock LP cover. They were a cool band signed to UNI Records by Russ Regan. They had a big hit record, 'Incense and Peppermints,' that DJ Dave Diamond on KBLA first spun. George ran around Sat Parush and tried everything on. Even dressing in the window. George also went outside and sat with some people on the street. Some knew who he was. He was totally cool about the whole trip.

"We all went to an Orange Julius stand and George had one of those to drink. Then we went to another clothes store on Santa Monica Boulevard called Siderial Time who had some of the grooviest clothes in the city. George wanted everything, and the owner, Larry, got him some special ribbon shirts that he loved just like the ones Larry did for the music group Lewis and Clark Expedition.

"The day ended, and we then went over to where I lived and talked for a little while. George invited me to come to San Francisco with him but I couldn't go. He promised to come back soon so we could do some more exploring together.

"During that time George stayed in L.A. Derek Taylor arranged for Ed Caraeff and I to attend the Ravi Shankar concert at the Hollywood Bowl. We drove in Ed's Mercedes-Benz, brown sedan four-door.

"At the Hollywood Bowl, we were given full access and sat with George on the side of the stage. No cameras and photos were allowed, but Ed managed to snap a photo with his

Nikon. No flash, very subtly, while George and I meditated to Ravi and his musicians doing a raga. I don't know how Ed did it with just available light.

**George Harrison and Rodney Bingenheimer
photo by Ed Caraeff**

"I next saw George a year later in Hollywood at Wallichs Music City one afternoon around the time when he was in town promoting the Beatles' *White Album* and did an interview on KPPC-FM in Pasadena. Many years later I ran into George and his second wife Olivia at a record company party, and they both knew all about my KROQ-FM radio show."

"It's not really a case of working for them or knowing them, because we all know, you know, in New Zealand or Madagascar they've just reached out and got us all hooked. Maybe not all, maybe that's generalizing, but they really are too much. There was always a thought they may be more than just people. And I would go along with that. They're the ones. They're the ones. Still are and I hope nobody objects to that.

"Esther Phillips' 'And I Love Her.' That was one of the best things that anyone ever did to a Beatles song. And, that's why they sent for her to appear on the show The Music of Lennon and McCartney that featured their music.

"In the end, you see, the Beatles music comes from the Beatles and there it lies and rests. And all the things they have and all the things that are envied by those who don't like them were given to them. Just because they were themselves. And all they've learned from all they've got is that they don't really need what they've got. So they're going on to other things. And we shall hear more of that, folks."

—DJ Derek Taylor, on his September 7, 1967, KRLA 1110 AM radio program

George Harrison was in Los Angeles for nearly a month and a half during October and November 1968 producing the Jackie Lomax debut *Is This What You Want?* Apple Records LP at Armin Steiner's Sound Recorders studio in Hollywood.

During his stay, a Capitol Records label executive handed him an advance lacquer pressing planned for the North American market of *The Beatles*, a/k/a the *White Album*. George was a bit miffed at the sound of the reference disc he heard, and not pleased by subtle changes in EQ and compression the mastering engineers at the U.S. company applied to the Abbey Road source tape.

So it was arranged for George over a two-day period to personally supervise a remastering process of a 2-track stereo tape at Capitol's facility on the premises.

On November 4th Harrison made a stop in Pasadena at underground radio station KPPC-FM, interviewed by DJs Charles Laquidara and Don Hall. On the broadcast Harrison discussed the impending Beatles Apple/Capitol product with the two jocks.

"It's really not like *Pepper* with that concept, you know. It's not really like that. It's more like a regular album, but it's a different thing altogether. It's on Apple. It's working fine, but there's quite a lot of work involved. But it's good, you know. The thing that comes out of it is good. It's worthwhile. There's plenty of good music, and we just try and keep it a high standard where everything is nice. It doesn't have to be a hit, I don't think, as long as it's good.

"I like so much different music. Otherwise you just get hung up doing one thing like the blues. And that's it for the rest of your life. Playing 12-bars. With our new album we've gotten much heavier. There is a blues track on it called 'Yer Blues.'"

At KPPC-FM, George was questioned about the Beatles' involvement with transcendental meditation and its founder, Maharishi Mahesh Yogi.

"The problem is—it's not really a problem, only if you make it a problem—the thing is that everything within the world is right and wrong and yes and no. Like good and bad. And good is held in its position by bad. You can only measure one by the other. But in actual fact they are both the same thing.

"So, really, Maharishi was great, you know. But there's a lot of things, and even down to the idea of doing *The Johnny Carson Show*. I mean, from one side of it you can accept everything. And from the other side you can't accept anything. It really depends. And I suppose we wanted, I realize still even now, I'd like the whole world to wake up and just to know who they are and what they're supposed to be doing and then it would be a great place.

"I thought that's why we really went along on a lot of things like the TV shows. I didn't mind too much the ideas of somebody like Maharishi going on TV. Even though it's

Part 3: Prick Up Your Ears

so out of the context. Even now, like this is the jet age, so we play jet-age-type music and like the way Maharishi was a jet-age yogi. And that can't be bad entirely. And it can't be good entirely. This is the terrible thing. The truth is something that isn't good or bad. It's beyond all that. And once you try and say what it is, then you bring yourself into that relativity that is good and bad, you know. It's really best just to find it yourself.

"From time to time I feel there's no difference between past, present and future. It's all the same."

Before departing the progressive underground stop, George signed off with a custom on-air station ID, "This is George Harrison of the Beatles at wonderful KPPC. Where the grass is greener in Pasadena. Thank you."

Harrison visited radio station KRLA on November 15, 1968 in Pasadena debuting selections live on the air with DJ Dave Hull from his now slightly tweaked acetate copy of *The White Album*.

After spinning "Yer Blues," Harrison teased the listeners with this wry comment, "You never knew we were really from Chicago, did ya? I mean, we learned all the basic blues rhythms and patterns when we were young lads living in Chicago. So we just thought we'd get back into it again." Harrison then introduced "Back in the U.S.S.R.," telling his rapt audience that "it reminds me a little of Brian Wilson."

After "Revolution No. 1" was tracked, Harrison commented, "That was recorded before the other side of 'Hey Jude.' Less attack. Not as much of a revolution. More of the Glenn Miller version."

About "Honey Pie," Harrison said, "This, I'm sure, a lot of the Hollywood people, the California people, will identify with this one. Very typical of that era."

After the initial airing of "Bungalow Bill," George told Dave Hull, "Bill is very interesting. Very interesting. We meet plenty of Bungalow Bills in our travels on the highway of life."

Regarding the numbers "Don't Pass Me By," "Rocky Raccoon," and "Piggies," Harrison back-announced, "Ringo wrote that one. Very nice. Ringo has always been very country-and-western-influenced. 'Rocky Raccoon' is very famous in our minds. I'm sure Rocky is the guy in all those westerns. 'Piggies' is written, really, two and a half years ago. It just seems funny that it's come out now."

After giving kudos to Ringo, Paul and John, Harrison, obviously well aware of the very recent and tragic June 1968 murder of Robert F. Kennedy in Los Angeles, slotted "Happiness Is a Warm Gun" and elaborated about the song's origins.

"'Happiness Is a Warm Gun' seemed to come by an American gun magazine after Kennedy, the second Kennedy, was killed. British newspapers printed ads for American gun mags. And one of the selling things was 'Happiness is a warm gun.'"

He then left the station after signing off with, "This is George Harrison. KRLA. Believe it or not."

On the evening of November 15th, Harrison, clad in a yellow shirt, green-striped pants and a leather jacket, also stopped by *The Smothers Brothers Comedy Hour* CBS-TV show in Television City to tape an introduction for the U.S. premiere of the Beatles' "Hey Jude" and "Revolution" film clips. The program was broadcast November 17th.

Bill Halverson in 1967 had assisted engineer Wally Heider on his remote recordings at the Monterey International Pop Festival, including Ravi Shankar's translucent performance.

Part 3: Prick Up Your Ears

Halverson in 1968 served as principal engineer on Cream's live album *Wheels Of Fire*, and had a regional history with the Beatles. "We also set up the stuff for the Beatles at the Hollywood Bowl in 1965. The Capitol engineers came in and got in the truck but we set it up. We brought the truck in. I had been around some noise."

During November 1968, Halverson engineered the Felix Pappalardi–produced Cream's recording session for "Badge" at Heider's Studio 3 in Hollywood, tracking George Harrison's rhythm guitar and Eric Clapton's lead part.

At the studio, attended by Jeannie Franklyn, a/k/a "Genie the Tailor," and Rodney Bingenheimer, covering the occasion for *GO* magazine, guitarists Harrison and Clapton were first introduced to a prototype Leslie foot pedal, courtesy of SIR (Studio Instrumental Rental). Harrison would soon employ the Leslie on the Beatles' *Let It Be*.

Halverson in 1969 would engineer the debut Crosby, Stills and Nash album and the first Eric Clapton solo LP. He would later engineer the mix down on a live Delaney Bonnie & Friends tape with guests Clapton and Harrison.

"In 1969 I presented onstage as the master of ceremonies the debut of John Lennon & the Plastic Ono Band with Yoko Ono, Alan White, Klaus Voorman, and Eric Clapton at the Varsity Stadium in Canada," reminds Kim Fowley.

"The Toronto Rock and Roll Revival. Chuck Berry, Jerry Lee Lewis, Gene Vincent, Little Richard and the Doors were on the show.

"I got the job because I was the voice of the Love-Ins in L.A. 1965, 1966, '67 and '68. I did some pop festival shows with the Doors, the Seeds, Jimi Hendrix and the Jefferson Airplane. I did all those shows and knew what to do with a large audience like 100,000 people. Ritchie Yorke, *Billboard* editor in Canada, and a contributor to *Rolling Stone* and NME—at the time he knew about me and persuaded the promoters to hire me. Four thousand dollars and a plane ticket.

"I also got a hotel room a week before the gig. My job was not only to announce the date but be a consultant and tell them how things were going.

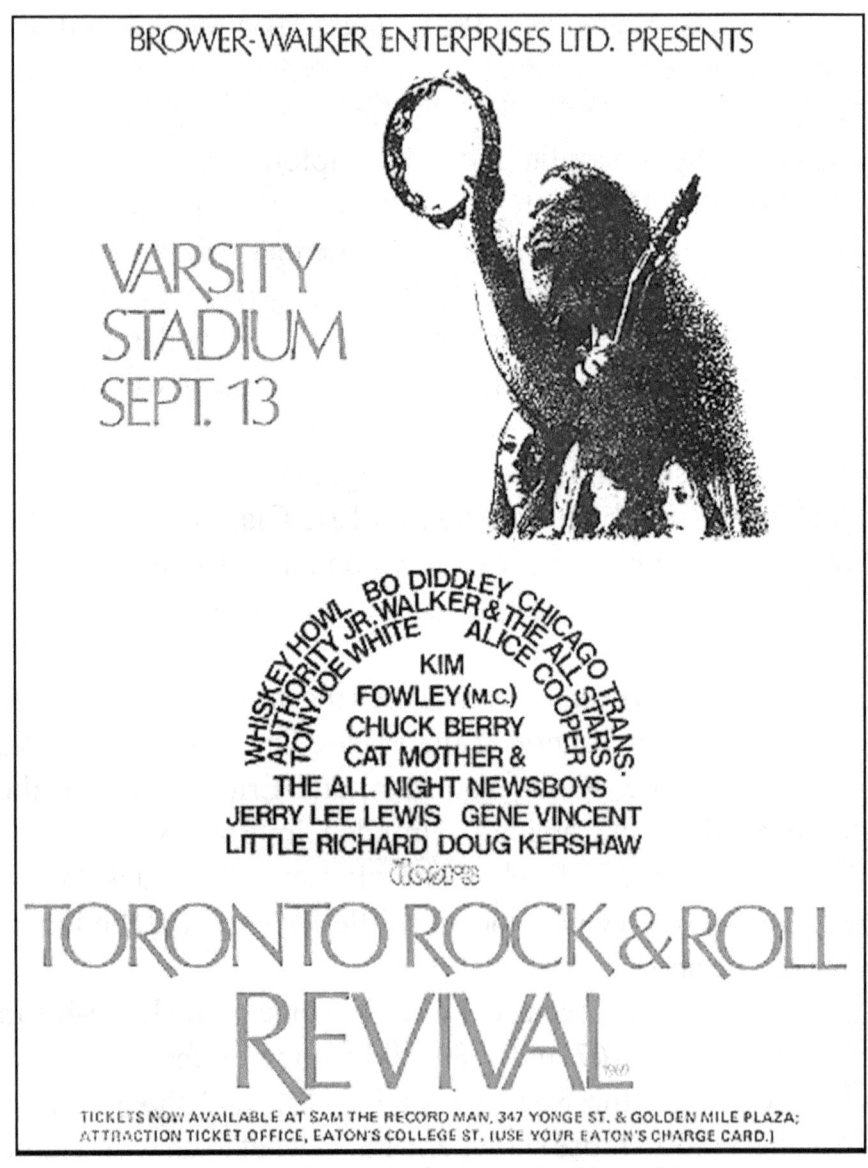

Flyer courtesy of Gary Pig Gold Archives

"We had a problem: We sold 2,000 tickets and no one was interested in coming to Canada from America via Detroit and the other cities. At the time, halfway through the week I met with the promoters, John Brower and Ken Walker, and Thor Eaton of Eaton's Department Store, who financed the thing. I told them to get John Lennon to show up. I said, 'The Beatles have just broken up, and John Lennon is the most competitive in the most competitive group. So call him up on a ploy level and invite him and Yoko on a chartered plane which Mr. Eaton can provide so they can sit at the show on a Royal Box kind of thing.'

"I wrote out the script, I had Derek Taylor training, and had met the Beatles a couple of times in England, once when John and Paul came to the hotel I was staying and promoting the soon-to-be-released *Pet Sounds* Beach Boys album. I knew the mentality to get a Beatle to show up.

"So, John Brower called Apple Records. Ritchie Yorke was with them and explained who I was that got them on the phone and heard the pitch. It was at a time when the Beatles would be at the Apple office. So John Lennon replied, 'I wouldn't feel right coming down there as a member of 'the Royal Family' just sitting there. I would want to play. Is it OK to play? I want to try out this thing I'm putting together with Eric Clapton, Yoko Ono, Alan White and Klaus Voormann.' So they sent the plane, and John and the band jammed and rehearsed on the way across the Atlantic.

"Yoko got sick on the way in. In the morning, all the Apple people from New York under Allen Klein's supervision were already bringing in the recording equipment. I don't think this was anyone exploiting John Lennon. I think John Lennon was a bright guy who called his then manager, Allen Klein, and told him to 'do the paper' with these promoters and make sure 'let's make a live album.' The recording stuff was all brought in, and then the documentary filmmaker D.A. Pennebaker came to film it.

"The chief of police in Toronto walked up to me and said, 'If there is a riot here, you will never leave Toronto alive.' That was pressure. The promoters said to me, 'When you do the live album, make sure to include our names in the intro.' They also were to pay me the other half of the $4,000.00 promised. So I had to juggle.

"Twenty thousand people showed up, and the big moment comes and the lights are blinding. Everything is on, and John Lennon summons me to the apron of the stage on the side by the canopy. I was dressed in a purple suit. He was in a white suit. This was not the time to have a MIDEM publishing-like discussion.

"I said hello to the Doors. Rodney Bingenheimer of *GO* magazine, who had picked up John and Yoko in a car at the airport with John Brower, was in the Plastic Ono Band dressing room. Gene Vincent and John exchanged autographs but John was really sick.

"Then John threw up. And he started to cry. He said 'I'm terrified. Imagine if you were in the Beatles as the only band you've only been in your life. The first time you are to step onstage with people that weren't in the Beatles. That's all you knew. Do something! Please do something so people won't know how afraid I am to go out there.' He went ahead of his band. They were behind him. He was in a bad way. So, I had seen a movie a decade before, in Catholic grade school, *Our Lady of Fatima*, where the Blessed Virgin appears in the sky and all the people light torches. So I figured, they all think John Lennon is God and this is a religious experience and a religious experiment. I said to myself, why don't I take this to the religious level subliminally by recreating *Our Lady of Fatima* with fire. Because if I said to the Varsity Stadium to please turn off the light and when I said the word 'Plastic Ono Band,' I want everybody to light matches simultaneously to welcome in a very friendly beatified way John and his friends.

"On the live album you'll hear 'Get your matches ready. Brower and Walker…present the Plastic Ono Band.' Twenty thousand matches were lit. It was a beautiful amber glow, and everyone let out a collective gasp and at that moment, Lennon, who was a Beatle, realized there's the moment that will take away from the nervousness of the moment and they went up to the stage and went right into 'Money.' And it was clear sailing from him and them all the way until the end. It seemed like an hour. Yoko sang in a bag," reported Fowley.

"The next day at Thor Eaton's house, where John and Yoko were staying with the Plastic Ono Band, I was sitting outside with the two promoters, and they were happy. 'Kim Fowley, you really earned your money. You're gonna be on the album, maybe there'll be a movie someday. Isn't life grand?'

"Then, Eric Clapton came out. I had known him from England at the Richmond Athletic Club days when he was in the Yardbirds. And I had met him again when Cream was forming. I had also danced a couple of months earlier onstage with Blind Faith in Inglewood at the Forum.

"At any rate, Eric and I connected. And he said, 'John and Yoko want to talk to you.' Eric escorted me to the sitting room of this mansion, and a very quiet John Lennon was sitting on the floor looking at Yoko on a Gandhi position. And Eric said, 'John and Yoko, Kim is here.' And I was delighted. 'Thanks for introducing us.' He was very gracious to me, and Klaus Voormann was in the room and so was Alan White.

"And I looked at Lennon and said, 'Can I ask you a question?' 'Yes.' 'Why did the Beatles break up?' The whole room stopped, and Lennon looked at me and said, 'May I give you an example?' 'Yes.' He said, 'You know 'Why Don't We Do It in the Road?' We were improvising on Canned Heat. We liked Canned Heat but didn't think they had enough humor. So we wrote that song as taking the Canned Heat formula and doing something else with it.

"'When the Beatles stopped writing favorite groups' efforts and their favorite groups' records, that's when the Beatles stopped being the Beatles.'

"He didn't mention all the things they've written about since. To him the Beatles ended because they didn't want to reinvent music they liked anymore. I told him to have a nice trip back. Goodbye. Never saw him again.

"When the album was released and my introduction was in there, and they ended it with the name Kim Fowley, my sex life improved 1,000%. To this day I can still get laid because my voice is on that record."

"John and Yoko Ono performing in Toronto. It's an amazing thing," filmmaker D.A. Pennebaker informed me in 2013.

"Coming at the end of that whole concert, it was the end of the Beatles. They understood it and at the end they fell silent. And John looked out and it was kind of scary and nobody was there. It was a funny moment. And they all left the stage and I remember a piece of paper blowing across the stage and slowly the audience came to life. I thought, 'My God. This is a fantastic wake.' Yoko was so crazy, but still, there was something so fascinating about what she did. You could see she did it with absolute conviction. What she was bringing to me was a kind of funeral cry for something that was lost. At the time I wasn't sure how I felt about it. But I did welcome it."

Part 3: Prick Up Your Ears

"What I remember most about Saturday, the 13th of September, 1969," recalls Gary Pig Gold, "was sneaking out of the house very early that morning, without my parents ever knowing, and hopping a train all the way into Toronto with the drummer from my rockin' teenage combo. Why? So I could buy my very first electric guitar, at a rundown pawnshop on the very wrong side of Church Street. It was red, cost $16.95, and we'd already arranged to hide it immediately afterwards at my drummer's house so my parents wouldn't find out.

"However, preparing our return to the nice quiet suburbs, we were surprised to suddenly hear music—*loud* music—in the air as we left the pawnshop. This was quite unusual in genteel 1969 Toronto, believe me. So we excitedly approached the source of the sound, and about a dozen blocks later found ourselves, alongside a few hundred others, outside Varsity Stadium. Yes indeed, something b-i-g seemed to be going on inside, and exploring the perimeter of the area we came upon an open gateway manned only, it seemed, by a very cool looking, shirtless 'dude,' as he'd be called nowadays. 'Wanna come inside?' But we had no tickets! 'C'mon, quick. Go in. I won't tell anyone,' cool guy laughed, motioning us forward.

Newspaper ad courtesy of Gary Pig Gold Archives

147

"But alas, my brand-semi-new $16.95 pride and joy hugged tightly under both arms, with only a cardboard box bound with elastic bands to protect it from the Revival inside, I declined. Regretfully. Even *more* regretfully it turned out when, safe at home the next morning, all the papers in town were screaming about how a Beatle, with some guy from Cream no less, had secretly flown all the way from London to play at Varsity Stadium."

ONE WHO WAS REALLY THERE

In 2012 engineer/producer Ken Scott published a memoir, written with Bobby Owsinski, *Abbey Road to Ziggy Stardust*.

In a 2012 phone interview Scott defined the reason he chose a role behind the console instead of singing in front of the microphone.

"The other thing is I know one of my own original things going into engineering is that I wanted to be a backroom boy. I didn't have the confidence or the desire to sort of be in the public eye or to be known or anything like that. I know it was a conscious effort on my part to do it that way. When I was at school working with the drama society I didn't want to be on stage. I wanted to be in the back helping to move everything along."

In his book, Scott, who worked under George Martin, reminisced about the first time he was in the control room with the Beatles in 1964.

Ken was booking tapes at the EMI studio library. He held the 4-track master tape of "Can't Buy Me Love" when it was being prepared as the next Beatles single.

He subsequently attended the "I Should Have Known Better" session, courtesy of engineer Norman "Hurricane"

Smith, and handclapped with Ringo and Paul for a take that wasn't used.

Scott's first day as a button pusher was June 1, 1964, during sessions for *A Hard Day's Night*. Songs not utilized in the film like "I'll Cry Instead" and "I'll Be Back" as well as "Matchbox" and "Slow Down."

Eventually Ken worked on *Help!* and *Rubber Soul*, before engineering the *White Album*.

"There were two feelings," relayed Scott to me in two 2013 phone conversations. "The first time I was actually in the control room with them I was like a fly on the wall and taking pictures. I was absolutely ecstatic. Excitement. 'My God. How did I ever get here?' That kind of thing. And if all ended tomorrow it would be worth it. And the first time working with them as button pusher and engineer it was pure fear. I had never done it before. Both as a button pusher and engineer I was thrown into the deep end. They were my first sessions.

"In working with the Beatles I got to experiment a lot and go through microphones and find out which mikes I liked for different things. So that moved on from there. Also, the learning experience with the Beatles is anything goes. It doesn't matter if it's a really bad sound as long as it fits.

"During the *White Album* period they were laying down the tracks and playing together, sorting out the arrangements together. It was all good. Obviously whoever wrote the song had more sort of sway over ideas than the others did. It was very much a group effort. Generally speaking the others would filter out whilst whoever's song it was worked on the finished thing. And it was like that for all of them. You knew that it would go a lot quicker with John than it would with Paul or George. Vocals would take the longest with Ringo. *[Laughs.]* Especially 'Good Night.'

"It was pretty much the same for all of them. I think very much the difference, writing-wise, for George, was that he was on his own. Even during the *White Album* there were times when Paul and John would interact on how a song should be. But George didn't have any of that. It was all him. And he didn't initially have the confidence in his songs. Even at the *White Album* stage. Yes, he was coming up with incredible stuff. He didn't know it yet."

Scott came up the ranks at Abbey Road from the mastering room. "The whole thing that one learned from the mastering, first and foremost, was what could go onto vinyl. Because you could put a lot more onto tape than you could on vinyl. You had to watch phase, you had to watch the amount of low end, all of that kind of thing, because it would make the stylus jump. That was really why they put you into mastering before allowing you to engineer. The other aspect of it that you learned was about EQ. Tone control. Bass, middle, high end and how you could affect that. What sounded good and what didn't sound good and how much it took to try and change a sound. After a few days you learned you could make it perfect just by adding one notch as opposed to piling it all on.

"I like the Beatles in mono because that was what they sanctioned. The whole point was, in England at the time, virtually no one had stereo. So it was pointless to do it in stereo because the core audience at home wouldn't hear it. They would only hear it in mono. Radio was basically AM at that point. There were record players. Not stereo systems or hi-fi systems. So, because of that, all we were interested in was the mono. The mixes, and that's why they only sanctioned the mono. Because no one else was gonna listen to it.

"And not until around *Magical Mystery Tour*, and by the *White Album*, they were totally into it. And the mono

White Album has some differences from the stereo. They were getting comments from fans in other countries saying, 'Did you realize there is this difference from the mono to the stereo?' And they thought they could sell twice as many records if they got involved making the stereos different."

I asked Scott to compare or contrast Abbey Road and Trident. The two studios he worked with the Beatles and George Harrison on *All Things Must Pass*. "Hey Jude" was done at Trident.

"Like Abbey Road, the control room at Trident was still above the studio where we were looking down," he explains. "So it was very much like Abbey Road number 2 studio in design. They were both great studios. There was something for me about number 2. The history of it. The whole thing. No matter how many times I go there I would stand at the top of those stairs and the hairs on the back of my neck would stand up. For me personally it has such a feeling. It's amazing.

"Comparing the two studios. Trident was much more laid back. It was young people. It wasn't the old people who ran Abbey Road. For musicians, Trident was a place to hang out. Whereas Abbey Road you only went in there when you had to kind of thing."

Richard Bosworth is a Beatles scholar and veteran music producer/engineer. In 2013 Bosworth produced and engineered Johnny Rivers at Capitol Studios in Hollywood. During 1991, Bosworth oversaw a Hollies recording session at Abbey Road Studio. He details one reason the Beatles' recordings, particularly their vocals, have sounded so good since 1962.

"Norman Smith, the first engineer, helped make them a hit. Regardless of his age at the time, he was a young engineer. Not a long-term staff guy at the Abbey Road, who happened to come along in an era and started doing things like closer microphone placements for the aggressive sounds. When you consider he went all the way through *Rubber Soul*. Incredible. Geoff Emerick took over for *Revolver*."

Bosworth points to one thing engineers Smith and Emerick had in common regarding their vocal-department duties. *Abbey Road* had a unique wind screener pop filter closer to the mike being the plosives where certain sounds would become very powerful and actually collapse the microphone capsule. You could get the vocalist closer to the microphone and a more in-your-face sound. They came up with a metal windscreen that had two different screens and two different meshes on them and different physical angles, where the one metal mesh was rounded and one was flat.

"The patterns of the mesh," he describes, "were diagonal to each other. Bolted tight onto the microphone, made with custom metal for *Abbey Road*. People started noticing quickly that moisture would get on the microphone capsule and you'd have to replace the capsule. Any pop filter changes anything to a certain extent. Unlike screen pop filters made out of foam, these were made out of metal and certainly not dampening high end. Those are unique.

"One of the other reasons the Beatles' recordings sound so good still to this day," Bosworth conveys, "is that the tape machine format was one-inch 4-track—a much wider tape width per track than any other analog tape format that has ever been conceived. The equivalent of 24-track would require that the tape format be six inches wide to get the same fidelity that the one-inch 4-track provided.

"The Beatles started with four tracks, moved to one-inch 8-track machine halfway during the *White Album*, and then *Let It Be* and *Abbey Road* were all recorded in one-inch

8-track format. Geoff Emerick engineered *Abbey Road* on a transistor recording desk.

"The Beatles worked with an incredible team of recording engineers." That includes Keith Grant and Eddie Kramer at Olympic Recording Studios, Barry Sheffield at Trident Recording Studios and Glyn Johns at Apple Recording Studios as well as Olympic, all located in London. That being said, the group recorded their greatest amount of work at EMI's Abbey Road Recording Studios, St. John's Wood, North London with [in chronological order] engineers Norman Smith, Geoff Emerick, Ken Scott and Phil McDonald.

"Norman Smith engineered virtually every studio performance of the band from 1962 through 1965. The iconic hits that Smith recorded encompass the singles, 'Love Me Do,' 'Please Please Me,' 'From Me To You,' 'She Loves You,' 'I Want to Hold Your Hand,' 'Can't Buy Me Love,' 'A Hard Day's Night,' 'I Feel Fine,' 'Eight Days a Week,' 'Ticket to Ride,' 'Help!,' 'Yesterday,' 'Day Tripper' and 'We Can Work It Out' and every LP from the Beatles' first, *Please Please Me*, to *Rubber Soul*.

"Many consider, Brian Wilson being one, *Rubber Soul* to be the paradigm shift for artistic achievement from the 45 to the LP. On *Rubber Soul*, Smith captured innovative new sounds such as fuzz bass guitar, sitar and distinctly dry vocals. To this day, when one listens to Norman Smith's recording of 'Ticket to Ride' on either radio, vinyl, CD, or MP3, it still lights up the speakers."

There isn't a music fan or a person on planet Earth who hasn't been profoundly inspired by engineer Geoff Emerick. From *Revolver* on, he was the full-time recording and remix engineer under George Martin. "Tomorrow Never Knows" was his first Beatles session. Geoff was behind the console until midway through the recording of the Beatles' *White Album*. He later returned to helm *Abbey Road*.

Emerick is, with Howard Massey, the author of *Here, There and Everywhere: My Life Recording the Music of the Beatles*. "I hear music in colors," he said to me many years ago at the Capitol Records Studio B.

"Bass and drums are always my favorite," Emerick stated. "And just building stuff around that, from color textures in my head, based upon what's happening in the studio."

Geoff's drum and bass sounds have motivated generations of musicians. His recording techniques and innovations include automatic double-tracking; backwards guitar solo and loops, and real-time varispeed manipulation that infused John Lennon's signature vocal echo.

On "Strawberry Fields Forever," Emerick executed the famed splice between the two versions of the recording, which were in different keys and tempos. He assembled the cinematic background to "Being for the Benefit of Mr. Kite" by putting together dozens of inch-long recordings of fairground organs and calliopes.

On September 9, 2009, the Beatles' entire original recorded catalogue, digitally remastered by Apple Corps Ltd. and EMI Music Marketing, was released worldwide, coinciding with the release of *The Beatles: Rock Band* video game.

In addition, the boxed set *The Beatles in Mono* was remastered by Paul Hicks and Sean Magee with Guy Massey and Steve Rooke.

As the mastering stage emerged, early vinyl pressings along with existing CDs were loaded into Pro Tools, thus allowing comparisons to be made with the original master tapes during the equalization process.

Part 3: Prick Up Your Ears

TISSUE REISSUE

Allan Rouse is the project coordinator of this monumental *The Beatles in Mono* undertaking.

Rouse joined EMI straight from school in 1971 at its Manchester Square head office, working as an assistant engineer in the demo studio. During this time he frequently worked with Norman "Hurricane" Smith.

In 1991, Rouse had his first involvement with the Beatles, copying all of their master tapes (mono, stereo, 4-track and 8-track) to digital tape as a safety backup.

That gig was followed by four years working with Sir George Martin as assistant and project coordinator on the TV documentary *The Making of Sgt. Pepper's* and the CDs *Live at the BBC* and *The Beatles Anthology*.

Further projects followed, including *The First U.S. Visit* and *Help!* DVDs and the albums *Let It Be...Naked* and *LOVE*, along with George Harrison's *Concert for Bangladesh* DVD and album. For a number of years, Allan has worked exclusively on Beatles and related projects.

Allan Rouse and Harvey Kubernik Interview.

Q: Can you tell me a bit about Norman "Hurricane" Smith and his contributions as an engineer on the initial Beatles sessions and your own EMI world with him starting in 1971? He engineered every Beatles recording through *Rubber Soul*.

A: Norman was a musician's engineer, and had formed his own band in the 1940s. So for the Beatles' early sessions, he understood that they had hardly any experience in a recording studio but a great deal in performing live, and that is the feel he wanted to capture. I believe the approach Norman took in recording them this way helped them settle into studio life and allowed them to perform in a way that made them feel the most relaxed, and I think it shows in their performances.

"I started at EMI's head office in 1971, where they had a small studio. Within a few days I was working as a tape op on Norman's follow-up single to 'Don't Let It Die.' I have to confess that I didn't know who he was even though he'd had a hit record, and I certainly wasn't aware of his past. This only transpired later after we had been chatting during one session and discovered that we lived a couple of miles from each other. After this he would call me in the control room at 5:30 when he was about to leave and ask if I wanted a lift. With an hour's journey we did a lot of talking and it was then that I learned about his work with the Beatles and Pink Floyd.

"On a few occasions I was lucky to record demos of his new songs, and with hindsight I now realize how lucky I was to be recording Norman on the very same equipment (Abbey Road provided Manchester Square with a 4-track mixing desk and 4-track tape machine) that he had used during the Sixties. This situation could have been intimidating, but Norman made me feel totally at ease despite the fact that I hardly had a clue what I was doing, but he never let on.

"Norman and I became good friends, and I was very happy when I was asked to interview him for an archive project only a few years ago. We spent two hours in Studio Two and finally finished the interview off at his home talking about his life as a musician, engineer, producer, artist and the 'good old days.' We also probably said a few times, 'It's not like it was in our day.'

Q: Do you remember in 1991 copying all the master Beatles tapes to digital, and what have been some of your feelings working on the new products?

A: By the time I started copying the Beatles' tapes, Abbey Road was already able to sync two 24-track analog machines together and also had 24- and 32-track digital machines. When I started copying their 4- and 8-track tapes and was able to isolate the different tracks, I was astonished at what they had been able to achieve, particularly when they started bouncing down (mixing) four tracks to another 4-track tape to allow them to do overdubs.

"In particular I think it illustrates the skills of the engineers and George Martin. The other thing that I remember vividly was isolating the vocal tracks; it was remarkable to listen to their unaccompanied voices, be it solo or as a group.

"Having listened to the multi-tracks in detail I had been made aware of the astonishing quality of the recordings. But one of the problems that was eventually encountered during the Sixties was too few tracks to record a song. So the engineer would mix the first four tracks of the recording to a new 4-track tape, but only using one or two tracks, leaving two or three for further overdubbing.

"We eventually devised a way of syncing these two 4-track tapes together, allowing us to then use the initial 4-track tape rather than the later mix-down with the overdub tape. This often gave us as many as seven instead of four tracks, and it is this practice that allowed us to remix in new stereo and surround sound for the film Yellow Submarine and subsequently the *Anthology* and *Help!* DVDs. Hearing the Beatles in surround is a unique experience and, because of the greater separation of tracks, permits you to hear the arrangements in a totally different way.

Q: Can you discuss working with Sir George Martin as his assistant and project coordinator on the TV documentary *The Making of Sgt. Pepper* and *Live at the BBC*? After being involved in the new Beatles' digitally remastered releases, is there even one more thing you learned or respected even more about what Sir George Martin contributed and brought into the sound of the Beatles' recordings?

A: Having managed to get a job at Abbey Road Studios and working on many sessions as a tape op, then eventually engineer, I thought that the closest I was ever going to get to a Beatles experience was being able to work in Studio 2. However, to sit in my room many years later with George Martin researching the Beatles' 4-track tapes for *Sgt. Pepper's* was as good as it gets. At the end of that job I had no idea that I was going to work with George again, and with the *Live at the BBC* I ended up spending many more months with him.

   "I think everybody learned a lot from each other during the sessions. It was a perfect combination of group, producer and engineers, but George's previous musical experiences brought something different to the Beatles' arrangements and productions that made them unique from other groups at the time.

Q: What do you notice about the digital world format you have overseen from the transfer of analog world and how it enhances the Beatles' catalogue in 2009 products?

A: Since the Beatles first appeared on CD in 1987, digital technology has improved a great deal, and the recent transfers now sound much closer to the master tapes. In addition, computer technology has allowed us to do things today that were previously hard or impossible to achieve, such as remove or improve technical issues such as tape drop-outs, bad edits, electrical clicks, vocal sibilance and microphone pops. I believe that the combination of the improved transfers and the removal of technical problems have allowed us to issue the catalogue in the best possible way since the albums' initial release.

"I have had the good fortune of working on a number of projects in recent years that have involved remixing to stereo and 5.1 surround with remarkable results by engineers Peter Cobbin, Paul Hicks and Guy Massey. But I still have the utmost admiration for the sound that the Beatles, Sir George Martin, engineers Norman Smith, Geoff Emerick, Ken Scott, Phil McDonald and Glyn Johns managed to achieve in the Sixties with recording technology in its infancy.

Q: What did you enjoy the most about the Beatles' *Anthology* sets?

A: Going through all the multi-track tapes for a second time with the added bonus of listening to them with the Beatles' producer, whilst Beatles engineer Geoff Emerick mixed the selected songs in another studio. However, one particular occasion will remain with me forever: when George Martin was joined by Paul, George and Ringo in Studio 2 to listen back to some of the alternative takes that had been selected.

"A few years later, we embarked on redoing the soundtrack to the video *Anthology* for DVD. This project to provide the whole soundtrack in surround sound and new stereo was done by a team of seven people and was spread over two years. At one point, both Studio 2 and 3 were working simultaneously for nearly three months; it was almost like the Beatles were back in the studios again, and it is rated as a career highlight by us all.

"There was something physical as well as audio that the analog medium communicated that digital never will,"

Steven Van Zandt emailed me in 2010. "It doesn't really matter of course unless you're listening to it on vinyl anyway and we know whatever they used will be a relief compared to the various, sometimes absurd, and usually terrible stereo versions.

"I had probably five lengthy conversations with [Apple Records'] Neil Aspinall over the last ten years of his life. In every one I begged him to put out the original configurations in the original mono. At first he couldn't quite understand why I was so passionate about it. By the third conversation he realized I was never going to stop bugging him about it and started seriously considering, not if, but when it could get done. He always had one distraction after the other, the Vegas thing took a lot of his time, but I'm sure he put it in motion before he left us. Anyway, I'm very very glad it got done.

"So now our masterpieces have been restored, and our leaders once again assume their proper place as our standard bearers. And peace returns to Pepperland."

Dr. James Cushing is thankful there are Beatles for sale (again) in mono formats.

"I'm glad that the Capitol boxes exist with the U.S. editions from a few years ago of the first American albums.

"Because Americans heard the Beatles that way and not the way the British box set will have. But as far as extras, embedded documentaries, the Capitol albums are in stereo and mono on one disc and it fits nicely. And I don't think that violates the original integrity of the album at all. Beatles in mono. That's the way the group originally mixed the music. To be heard out of a small speaker, and because most record players in 1963 and '64 were mono. 1963-1965. Stereo was for weirdo audiophiles.

"In mono you get a more blended sound. One gets the sense you are hearing a single source coming at you. The emphasis is the organic singleness of the music. And with the stereo, sometimes the mixes give a little too much distance between instruments. The voices on one side and the instruments on the other. So you hear things with a little too much space between them. Although that situation improves as the stereo mixes improved in quality."

Since it was recorded, the Beatles' music has been heard on a variety of configurations, from chunky reel-to-reel tapes and 8-track cartridges to invisible computer files. But there has never been a more romantic or thrilling medium for music than a long-playing 12-inch disc. We *play* records. The process of carefully slipping the disc out of the sleeve, cleaning it and lowering the stylus provides a personal involvement in the reproduction of the music.

When the Beatles' albums were first released, the listener enjoyed a tangible relationship with the music in the grooves of a record. There was an emotional connection to the artifact carrying the sound, and this bond was strengthened by the LP sleeve. Rather than a merely functional object to protect the disc, it was elevated to a stylish accessory. Certainly, the cover of a Beatles album transmitted a message about the music it was wrapped around.

For example, the dominant orange and brown hues and elongated faces on the front of *Rubber Soul* seem to embody the sound of the record. With the advent of the cassette tape in the Seventies and the compact disc in the 1980s, album artwork was reduced in size and importance, losing much of its charm. That is partly why vinyl LPs have not, as predicted, been discarded.

None of that would really matter, of course, were it not for the enduring power of the Beatles' music.

In September 2009, the Beatles' remastered albums on CD graced charts around the world. Seventeen million album sales within seven months provided resounding evidence of the timeless relevance of their legacy. Through five decades, the music of the Beatles has captivated generation upon generation.

Dr. James Cushing has additional reasons why this remastered Beatles catalog was so logical for re-release.

"It's that we are currently enjoying a vinyl revival. As recent as 2010, vinyl was the fastest growing format; in 2011 U.S. vinyl sales topped 3.6 million sales, a 37% increase from the previous year. And it's grown in the last three years. Why is this happening? Because people want greater personal involvement with the process of listening to recorded music.

"Recall the situation of the vinyl listener. You put the vinyl disc down on a turntable, where it can be clearly seen, and you turn a switch that causes the disc to rotate. As the music plays, you get to look at a rotating disc. There is something about watching an object rotate that is attractive, calming, and fundamentally interesting.

"Then there is the question of the stylus," claims Dr. Cushing. "You must clean it and place it manually on the record. You hear that unique clicking sound that the needle makes when it goes into the record. And then you hear that special, amplified silence in the groove before the music starts. When the diamond stylus vibrates in the record, the vinyl is actually melting a little bit from the pressure of the diamond. And that melting is what enables the needle to translate the liquid in the grooves to physical sound.

"So there is a mysterious quality in all vinyl records. At the same time, the technology is transparent. With compact discs, all you see is track numbers.

"The vinyl technology also demands that you alter your sense of time to fit the experience. The music starts but only continues for 15 or 20 minutes. You are forced to turn the LP over, not just stare at numbers on a CD player source and push buttons."

About the "message" in these Beatles mono and stereo CD boxes, and now these stereo vinyl LPs, Dr. Cushing contends, "these mysterious objects have returned. But they have returned with a new meaning. The first time we played and absorbed these Beatle LPs, a long, long time ago, they related to a terribly exciting phenomenon, strange yet familiar, of a mood and a sensibility that was happening at that very moment, somewhere in actuality, and being captured in world-historical music.

"Today, the LPs are a monument to what these four people (five if you include George Martin) accomplished in that mood, when the greatest aspirations of the Sixties were completely believed. People don't believe those things anymore but they want to know that there was a time when they were believed.

"I wish I could be listening to the Beatles' records for the first time," laments Dr. Cushing. "They're so filled with associations, memories, psychological and emotional things, to be able to hear the songs just as songs must be a remarkable experience now. And it's real great that this new set has greatly improved sound so that people will be able to really enjoy it."

I asked the professor: Is it the enthusiasm, the freshness, the profound affirmation of life, plus that mysterious element that makes the recordings memorable and exciting?

"Maybe, but why their music has durability is because it existed primarily in terms of itself. Not primarily in terms as a motor to propel a financial empire. With the Beatles there was no sprit of calculation. There is a spirit of openness and sincerity. Which was immediately appealing and unpretentious.

"Paul and John's magic was that they were close. They also grew apart. Which is a paradox of this whole thing, as best demonstrated on the *White Album*. The Lennon and McCartney scope of songs were to become more experimental and built on the fundamental confidence that they always had. They both believed musically they could do anything they wanted to and aided by the belief that never died.

"They still grip us, and it may have something to do with our investment of our own personal history in them. My son Alex, age 17, has lived in a world where the Beatles has always been in the past.

"I didn't buy the stereo vinyl box set," boasts Dr. Cushing. "Because I waited for the mono configurations that came out, announced for 2013. I think the stereo mixes of the Beatles' early CDs are terrible. The vocals are on one side and the instruments are on the other. The mono CDs give a much more realistically musical experience."

"Don't forget," DJ, actor, author and music historian Roger Steffens interjects, "hearing the early work of the Beatles, particularly 1963 and 1964, and in recent *Red* [1962–1966] and *Blue* [1967–1970] Beatles albums, it detached them from their original context to an American audience.

"We absorbed the Beatles' catalogue in a very different way from the British. We have to talk in geographic terms when we are trying to make some sense of this stuff. So these albums are detached and thrown together in a way that was different from the way an album was tracked. With great taste, and a sense of build, action and momentum.

"The magic of the Beatles," emphasizes Steffens, "was that everything sounded different from what came before. And that was a conscious choice on their part. George Martin mentioned as the fifth Beatle doesn't begin to cover it."

To commemorate the 50th anniversary of the Beatles history-making U.S. Albums, a new 13 CD Beatles collection spanning 1964's *Meet The Beatles!* to 1970's *Hey Jude*, was released January 21, 2014 in North America by Apple Corps Ltd./Capitol. The Beatles' U.S. albums differed from the band's U.K. albums in a variety of ways, including different track lists, song mixes, album titles, and art.

The albums are presented in mono and stereo, with the exception of *The Beatles' Story* and *Hey Jude*, which are in stereo only. Collected in a boxed set with faithfully replicated original LP artwork, including the albums' inner sleeves, the 13 CDs are accompanied by a 64-page booklet with Beatles photos and promotional art from the time, as well as a new essay by American author and television executive Bill Flanagan.

For a limited time, all of the albums (with the exception of *The Beatles' Story,* an audio documentary album) will also be available for individual CD purchase. *A Hard Day's Night* (Original Motion Picture Soundtrack), *The Beatles' Story, Yesterday And Today, Hey Jude*, and the U.S. version of *Revolver* make their CD debuts with these releases.

In October of 2013, I was invited to a Genesis Publications event in Hollywood held at the Arch Light Theater on Sunset Boulevard to launch the worldwide premiere of Ringo Starr's limited-edition book *Photograph.*

In the Genesis Publications product publicity materials (RingoPhotoBook.com) for *Photograph*, Starr divulged, "As a drummer, not having a car was pretty difficult. When I had to come on the bus, I had to beg drummers in the other bands, 'Let me play your drums.' Sometimes they'd let me and sometimes they wouldn't. Later on, when I got my car, other drummers would beg me, 'Let me use your kit, man!' and I'd say, 'Sure,' because I knew what begging for a kit was all about.

"We made some incredible music. There were many magic moments when it really worked. When you're together, the band is together and the audience is together, it creates a magical, spiritual moment. It's a good reason to go on tour."

Inside the venue, the beaming Beatle in the room proudly admitted in a stage conversation with Melinda Newman of *Billboard* magazine that, "Jim Keltner is my favorite drummer. He was interviewed, and he said, 'Charlie Watts is the best rock drummer in the world.' So I called him. 'You thought Charlie Watts was the best rock drummer?' And he said, 'Ah…But Ring. You swing.' And I do. And I got that from my big band music. I don't know where that came from."

Drummer Clem Burke, co-founder of Blondie, certainly agrees with Keltner. "The Beatles are the soundtrack of my generation. They are and always will be my muse. I'll listen to a few songs before a show and get a rush of emotions. They had the best drummer in rock 'n' roll that really made the recordings swing. They were the natural progression from the roots of the music. The early recordings spread the gospel of Little Richard, Buddy Holly, and Motown to a new generation of rockers."

"I could talk all day about how the Beatles influenced me," Foo Fighters Dave Grohl exclaimed at the same

October 2013 media and friends gathering for Ringo Starr's *Photograph* book. And he merrily did.

"Honestly, when I was young and discovered the Beatles, one of the things that I loved about them so much was that each one of them had such distinct personalities that, you know, like George just made you play the guitar, and John made you want to scream and Paul made you want to play everything. But Ringo, really, was the first time that I listened to music and really focused on the drummer. I don't mean the way he played but as a personality. And to me that should determine the way that he played drums. Like, when I listen to a drummer it's almost like listening to them speak. I think that drummers should show their sense of humor and their sense of passion. 'Cause it's all in their hands, you know. It's in your heart and your hands. So nobody plays drums like Ringo. Because he's Ringo."

"Ringo was a great drummer," states Ken Scott. "Still so many people fail to realize that he was an incredible rock drummer. For me, it's from his lack of technical knowledge. It was all feel for him. I'm of the opinion that he would go into a fill not knowing how he was ever going to get out of it. And halfway through he suddenly realized he has to get out of it, so come up with some unique way to get out of that fill.

"It's much like all of the Beatles, they all grew so much as musicians. As technicians. During the short life of the Beatles. Ringo did as well. He was an incredible drummer and great to work with. All of them."

"I had this conversation with [Jim] Keltner one time," continues Dave Grohl, "where we sat and we talked about drumming. Keltner, who, you know, obviously, is one of the greatest drummers of all time. He was like, 'Man, I try. I try so hard. I try and do what he does. And I just can't do it.'

"And to think honestly, because that's the way he is. And he's become a great reference I'm sure. Any musician knows that when you're in the studio and you want that specific thing, you just say, 'Hey. Do that Ringo thing.' But you know exactly what it means. And to me that's always been like the goal—is to be the drummer where someone says, 'Hey. Do that thing that guy…'

"My introduction to music really was the Beatles. I think I was maybe six or seven years old and I got the records. And I had this little guitar, and my mother bought me this book, a complete Beatles anthology [of] chord charts. I would put records on and learn these chords. The Beatles taught me how to play music. The records. Book and guitar. And so that became the foundation of everything that I understood musically from then on. Whether it was arrangement, harmony, or tempo or whatever it was. It all began there. So, in listening to the drum, that becomes your reference point. It became my reference point for everything, you know. 'Oh, that guy is too busy.' 'Oh, that guy doesn't have any grooves.' 'Add this in the middle.' 'That song is too long.' The Beatles are my reference. That's just how I related to everything.

"Like, when I was in Nirvana the last thing in the world I wanted to do was complicate that songwriting process. Because Kurt [Cobain] was brilliant. He wrote great songs, and I looked at it, what I need to do in that band as it needed to do what Ringo did in so many songs, which was lay it down. Let the song happen. Just lay it down and do your thing. But there was that part of me that, like, I want to sing. I wanted to do my own thing. I never really considered myself a showman, and to swing either, but when I would watch Ringo sing a song or play the drums it just kind of seemed so effortless. Because it was coming from a real place. And that to me is what being a musician should be. Not to really force it so much but rather just kind of let it kind of happen. Just be yourself," imparted Grohl.

"Honestly, when I listen to those recordings, it's funny, because to me those recordings are almost like sonic photographs. With the camera you're trying to capture that moment in time. And it's the same thing with music. And if you're in the studio and recording tape, you're trying to capture that moment so that it lives forever. The sound of what you did that afternoon. Like I said. It's all in your hands and in your heart. So there's kind of no use trying to sound like anyone else. 'Cause you just can't. That's the way they do it. And fortunately it sounded the way he did and the way he does. That's him.

"I like rockers. I love the pretty stuff, too. But when I listen to a song like 'Hey Bulldog,' or some of the heavier ones, those are the ones where the grooves were down. I don't know how the hell you got those drum sounds, man. But there's a lot of those moments where there is air between the fills and those fills sort of roll into the next section. Those are things that people spend lifetimes trying to get and capture those moments."

In October 2010, EMI/Cap Records reissued George Harrison's 1970 solo debut, *All Things Must Pass* remastered and restored in a limited edition, numbered 3 LP vinyl collection commemorating the album's 40th anniversary. The album was newly remastered at Abbey Road Studios from the original analogue master tapes.

Originally released November 27, 1970, *All Things Must Pass*, co-produced by Harrison and Phil Spector, engineered by Ken Scott, topped the *Billboard* Top 200 chart for seven weeks and spawned the international #1 single, "My Sweet Lord."

Scott started engineering for the Beatles in the middle of their *Magical Mystery Tour* album and present on the mix for "I Am the Walrus." He subsequently engineered the Beatles' *White Album*.

"On that album George Harrison was really coming into his own," believes Scott. "From the number of his songs on this album collection and other tunes he was developing that would surface on his solo album *All Things Must Pass*.

"During that period they were laying down the tracks and playing together, sorting out the arrangements together. It was all good. Obviously whoever wrote the song had more sort of sway over ideas than the others did. It was very much a group effort. Generally speaking the others would filter out whilst whoever's song it was worked on the finished thing. And it was like that for all of them. You knew that it would go a lot quicker with John than it would with Paul or George. Vocals would take the longest with Ringo. *[Laughs.]* Especially 'Good Night.'

"If you think about it, he gave 'My Sweet Lord' away to Billy Preston. There was something he wanted to give away to Jackie Lomax. He didn't have the confidence within himself to do those songs. Like 'Not Guilty,' even then, we never completed it. We never really got it to the point where it was even sort of even considered going on the album."

PART 4: SAVE THE TIGER

During a 1997 interview I conducted with George Harrison printed in *HITS,* he outlined the Beatles' studio expeditions to me.

"That was the environment in the band—everybody was very open to bringing in new ideas. We were listening to all sorts of things, Stockhausen, avant-garde music, whatever, and most of it made its way onto our records.

"A man from the Asian Music Circle in London arranged a meeting between Ravi [Shankar] and myself. Our meeting has made all the difference in my life. The sitar is an instrument I've loved for a long time. For three or four years I practiced on it every day. But it's a very difficult instrument, and one that takes a toll on you physically. It even takes a year to just learn how to properly hold it. But I enjoyed playing it, even the punishing side of it, because it disciplined me so much, which was something I hadn't really experienced to a great extent before."

Harrison had first heard the sitar on the set of *Help!* Later that same year, he would record with the instrument on John Lennon's "Norwegian Wood (This Bird Has Flown)." Subsequently, Harrison integrated the sitar into his own composition "Love You To" for the Beatles' *Revolver* album. He fused sitar and Indian influences on his selection "Within You Without You" on the influential *Sgt. Pepper's Lonely Hearts Club Band* album and also on "The Inner Light," the obscure B-side to the "Lady Madonna" single.

Harrison went on to describe his earliest attempt at playing the sitar with the Beatles as "very rudimentary. I didn't know how to tune it properly, and it was a very cheap sitar to begin with. So 'Norwegian Wood' was very much an early experiment. By the time we recorded 'Love You To,' I had made some strides."

"George Harrison in the Angel City" by Kirk Silsbee

George Harrison is credited with bringing Indian music and Ravi Shankar to the attention of the larger public, through his sitar playing on "Norwegian Wood," "Tomorrow Never Knows" and "Within You Without You." That story has an almost mystical Los Angeles angle to it.

Beginning in the late 1950s, Dick Bock had been recording Ravi for his World Pacific label, and despite poor sales, that music became the private reserve for a handful of influential tastemakers. Ben Shapiro, another bohemian impresario, booked Shankar at his Sunset Strip nitery the Renaissance and presented him in concerts. Jazz flutist Paul Horn, a proto–New Ager who led the Renaissance house band, guested on *Ravi's Portrait of a Genius* album. Shankar's music was a tough sell to American audiences, but Bock and Shapiro evangelized on his behalf. It was Bock who introduced Shankar to John Coltrane, and the two masters had some very fruitful and provocative meetings. John Tynan, Los Angeles correspondent for *Down Beat* magazine, published a Shankar feature in May of 1965.

Byrds manager Jim Dickson brought David Crosby to a Shankar recording session in early 1965, and Crosby was soon raving about Ravi to the *KRLA Beat*. The Beatles came to town for a Bowl concert in August, and John Lennon and

Harrison hung out with Roger McGuinn and Crosby. Maybe it was the acid or maybe it was the bubbling hot tub, but the experience of hearing a Ravi Shankar record for the first time had a profound effect on Harrison.

The Byrds brought a synthesis of Coltrane, Shankar and Bach in "Eight Miles High" to the Top 40 at the beginning of 1966—six months before Harrison first heard Ravi live at a London concert. Ben Shapiro was responsible for getting Shankar on the bill at the Monterey International Pop Festival, and he was the only performer who was paid. The $5,000 fee went into the opening of Shankar's Kinnara Music School on Robertson. Doors Robby Krieger and John Densmore and future Little Feat founder Lowell George studied there. Harrison was onstage during Shankar's Hollywood Bowl concert in the summer of 1967 and he used his Beatle cachet to boost Kinnara through an on-site press conference. Shapiro presented Shankar for years after the Monterey triumph in concerts up and down the California coast.

But before Del Shannon, the Turtles and Rick Nelson recorded with sitars, and before Carnaby Street boutiques sold "sitar jackets," and before Paul Horn accompanied the Beatles on their Maharishi Mahesh Yogi retreat, deejay Humble Harve captured the pop exotica feel of the moment over KBLA one Sunday night. His stream-of-consciousness rap over the pulsating instrumental ending of "Mystic Eyes" by Them contained the following: "Ummm, UNNHH, baby! I never seen anybody with a pair uh eyes like you got, baby. Those pupils are sure…bulgin' out tonight. Yey-yah. Guess you could call 'em mystic eyes. They look like somethin' Ravi Shankar brought in, baby, then forgot to take out again. It's 10:19, KBLA-Around-the-World-Sweepstakes-Time-in-the-City-of-the-Angels...

In the mid-Seventies when I was writing a weekly music column for *Melody Maker*, George Harrison invited me to attend a Ravi Shankar sound check and show at the Roxy Theater. George was proudly showcasing his special Dark Horse Records/A&M label artist.

**Ravi Shankar at the Monterey Pop Festival, June 1967
photo by Henry Diltz**

"He's a very rare person," Ravi Shankar insisted to me twenty years later in a 1997 *HITS* Magazine interview at his home in Encinitas, California. "It is something so special. There are many other people who could do what George does, but they don't have that depth. He's so unusual. What has clicked between him and me, what he gets from me, and what I get from him, that love and that respect and understanding from music and everything, is really the most important thing. It's not the money, or he helping me to record; that's not the main thing. But it's the very special bond between both of us."

"Ray [Manzarek] had a previous relationship with World Pacific Records in 1965 when he was on the label with

Part 4: Save the Tiger

Rick and the Ravens and recorded for Dick Bock, who owned the label, and released Ravi Shankar albums in the U.S.," Doors co-founder and drummer John Densmore related to me in a 2008 *MOJO* interview. "We got a couple hours of free studio time at World Pacific recording studios, and that's when we got to make a demo in 1965.

"On the way into the studio Ravi Shankar is leaving with Alla Rakha, my idol—who I didn't know was going to be my idol yet—was on the way out with these little tabla drums, which I soon find out by studying at the Kinnara School are the most sophisticated drums in the world. I'm in awe of them. It's the East! And I'm just a surfer. Not literally, but from West L.A.," chuckled Densmore.

"Robby [Krieger] and I went to Ravi Shankar's Kinnara School of Indian Music. When you're students at the Kinnara School of Music, you get to sit onstage with the master at UCLA's Royce Hall. Later Robby and I go see Ravi play at the Hollywood Bowl, and George is on stage. Ravi didn't teach at the school, but he'd drop in and give a little lecture on 'Sublimating Your Sexual Drive Into Your Instrument.'

"Transcendental Meditation glued together myself, Ray, Robby and Jim [Morrison]. I don't know if you know this story. Jim didn't meditate; Robby and I went and Ray was there. That's where we met. One time Jim came and he wanted to look into Maharishi's eyes…and Jim later said, 'Well, he's got something. I'm not gonna meditate but he's got something.' This was the first class in the country. We were two years ahead of the Beatles, thank you. *[Laughs.]*

"The very first TM class was with Clint Eastwood and Paul Horn the year before me. Paul later was in India with the Beatles.

"We were starting our second album, *Strange Days,* when our engineer Bruce Botnick, got an advance copy of *Sgt.*

Pepper's before it was released and played it for us. Oh, what a challenge... OK. So, *Strange Days*, we were definitely more into experimental because of hearing that album, but we didn't want to do horns and strings, but it was so wild. Ringo did 400 pounds of overdubs on that album.

"I saw Ringo at the opening of the Beatles' *LOVE* show in Las Vegas. I had to tell him how much I had admired the Beatles. His feel was it. People give him shit all the time. I don't know, but as one drummer to another it felt real good to say, 'Man, I just dug your feel.'

"We weren't in competition with the Beatles. When I think competition, it's sonic competition. Lennon and McCartney then were more semi-traditional songwriters, and we were West Coast acid heads. But sonically, we were challenged, and started to do backward piano tracks. 'The recording studio is the fifth Door. Let's experiment.' That's what *Sgt. Pepper's* did. We didn't try and copy Lennon and McCartney. George Harrison came to one of the *Soft Parade* sessions."

"In 1967 I was invited to attend the Ravi Shankar press conference at the Kinnara School of Music," muses Henry Diltz. "George was there. I took photos there and haven't found them since. Ravi at the time was the soundtrack of Laurel Canyon. And there is a relationship between the banjo and the sitar. They have drone strings, like a bagpipe. There is one note that plays over and over again, which is banjo. It's the fifth string. It was in mountain modal music. And it was kind of head trippy, you know.

"I saw Ravi at the Monterey International Pop Festival. George's devotion to Ravi was heartwarming. We were all discovering India. Ravi's records were always played in Laurel Canyon with lots of incense curling in the air. And it was sort of psychedelic. And then we were reading *Autobiography of a Yogi*. And so we were all things India. A place that was looming, a very deep and interesting and informative world."

The impact of Ravi Shankar was not lost on songwriter and record executive Russ Titelman, who produced albums by Little Feat and George Harrison.

"I was getting to know Lowell George at the time of *Performance* in 1969 that sorta led to Warner Bros. as a full-time thing. See, Lowell George, who worked uncredited on the *Performance* soundtrack, was a big fan of Ravi Shankar.

"Shankar had opened a school, the Kinnara School of Music, and I met Lowell there because I was studying sitar there for a year. Although I couldn't play sitar that well, Lowell could. Incidentally, George Harrison, who I would later produce, also came by and we were introduced. So Lowell and I got close and drove around all the time in this Morgan car he had. Lowell was amazingly talented.

"He was a flute player in high school, and he knew how to play Japanese *shakuhachi* flute; anything he picked up he could figure out, and he of course was a truly great guitar player. As we were studying sitar, Jack Nitzsche was doing this *Performance* movie score with all sorts of different instrumentation, and I said, 'Look, we'll have tamboura and veena,' which I borrowed from the school."

August 1st is the anniversary of two landmark 1971 benefit concerts that nearly 40,000 people attended at Madison Square Garden in New York City featuring George Harrison, Ravi Shankar, Bob Dylan, Leon Russell, Billy Preston, Badfinger, Eric Clapton and Ringo Starr, among others.

It was in Los Angeles earlier that summer when Harrison was alerted to the scale of suffering his friend and sitar teacher

Shankar was feeling about the struggle for independence for the 10 million East Pakistani refugees who had fled over the border from West Pakistan to neighboring India to escape mass starvation, hunger, and death. Nearly 3 million people were killed. The dilemma and crisis was deepened when the 1970 Bhola cyclone and floods hit the region. At that moment, very little monies and help were made available from foreign governments.

**George Harrison Bangla Desh Message
photo by Henry Diltz**

Part 4: Save the Tiger

Harrison organized two relief-of-refugees charity concerts while composing, recording and releasing a studio single, "Bangla Desh," that was available just before the heralded affair.

At the performances, Harrison and his karmic pals offered stellar efforts of "Wah-Wah," "Here Comes the Sun," "Something," "While My Guitar Gently Weeps," "My Sweet Lord," "Just Like a Woman," "Blowin' in the Wind" and "A Hard Rain's A-Gonna Fall."

The shows were recorded by Phil Spector and engineer Gary Kellgren with the music produced by Spector and George Harrison. Production coordination was done by Jon Taplin, Steve Lieber and Allan Steckler. Staging and lighting were courtesy of Chip Monck Enterprises and Bruce De Forrest.

The two concerts were successful, garnering U.S. venue proceeds of $243,418.50 donated to UNICEF while also raising awareness and visibility for the organization around the world.

The Concert for Bangladesh (originally spelled, as the nation originally was, as *Bangla Desh*) was commercially released as a triple album in retail outlets just before Christmas 1971 in the U.S. and after New Year's Day 1972 in the U.K. It immediately became a best seller, landing at No. 2 for several weeks in the U.S. charts and becoming Harrison's second No. 1 U.K. album. The set won the Grammy for Album of the Year of 1972 for producers Harrison and Phil Spector.

The concert also became a film, directed by Saul Swimmer, who had served as co-producer of the Neil Aspinall- and Mal Evans-produced *Let It Be* documentary in 1970.

Eventually millions of dollars were given to UNICEF, who distributed milk, blankets and clothing to refugees.

George Harrison set up his own charity foundation, the George Harrison Fund for UNICEF, after he became frustrated with red tape and bureaucracies that had slowed down the process of spreading monies intended for recipients. The fund, overseen by his wife Olivia, has generated millions of dollars to help others dealing with natural disasters, malnutrition and other emergencies. Donations can be made online at *www.GeorgeHarrisonFundForUNICEF.com*.

Apple Corps/Capitol in October 2005 released *The Concert for Bangladesh: George Harrison and Friends* on DVD and CD in anticipation of the 35th anniversary of this collaborative event. The 2-DVD package was issued by Apple Corps/Rhino and the expanded 2-CD set by Apple Corps/Capitol. The DVD includes the original 99-minute film restored and remixed in 5.1, as well as 72 minutes of extras.

There is also previously unseen footage: "If Not for You," with George and Bob Dylan from rehearsals, "Come On in My Kitchen" featuring George, Eric Clapton and Leon Russell at the sound check, and a Bob Dylan performance from the afternoon show of "Love Minus Zero/No Limit," not included in the original film.

The extras feature a 45-minute documentary, *The Concert for Bangladesh Revisited* with George Harrison and Friends," about the background to the event, with exclusive interviews and contributions from Sir Bob Geldof and United Nations Secretary-General Kofi Annan, who stated, "George and his friends were pioneers."

The album of the concert has been remixed and repackaged, and contains an additional track of Bob Dylan performing "Love Minus Zero/No Limit."

The Concert for Bangladesh was one of the first benefit shows, along with the 1967 Lou Adler–and John Phillips–produced Monterey International Pop Festival nonprofit venture, that brought together an extraordinary assemblage of major artists collaborating for a common humanitarian cause—setting the precedent that music could be used to serve a higher purpose. The Concert for Bangladesh has been the inspiration and forerunner to the major global fundraising events of recent years, preceding Live Aid by 14 years.

All artists' royalties from the sales of the DVDs and CDs continue to go to UNICEF.

George Harrison and master sitar musician Ravi Shankar met in early summer 1971 in Los Angeles, where they birthed the idea for the concert.

"I told George, and George wanted to help me," Shankar explained to me in his San Diego–area home in a 1997 interview published in *HITS* magazine. "The film *Raga* was ready and it needed some finishing in which George helped. It was released, I believe, in 1972."

Shankar lived in Los Angeles in 1971. "I had a house. A beautiful Spanish villa. And at that time George was in town, and at that time I was planning to do a benefit concert for Bangla Desh, because I was very hurt that this whole thing was going on. To help this refugee problem, I wanted to raise some money. Everybody, every Indian, was thinking about doing that. And then, when I thought about it, I knew I could do more than any other Indian musician. Still, how much can you send? $20,000? $25,000, at the most?"

"At this time of turmoil I was having, George was there," pleaded Ravi comically in our *HITS* conversation. "He came to meet me and I was sitting. He saw me. From 1966, whenever he came to town, we would meet. At that time, he was staying in L.A. for a couple of weeks. I told him what I was planning. You know, it's like a drop in the ocean. At the same time, I never wanted to take advantage of him. I did not want to say, 'Would you help me?' But, somehow, it came very naturally. He was so sympathetic. 'Well...let's do something.' And you know that made me feel so happy. What he did, he immediately started phoning and booking things up. He phoned and got Madison Square Garden.

"Later, he contacted Bob Dylan, Eric Clapton, Billy Preston and a few of his friends. Somehow, it was done. Within three weeks or so, we gave a performance and it was sold out. So, they had to schedule a matinee. As you know, the first half was me. I called my guru's son Ali Akbar Khan, who plays the sarod. We were the first part. I composed the first lines for the items played as we always do and we improvised. And then intermission. There was no clapping when we were tuning, which is seen in the film and the people were so well-behaved. A lot of matches. It went beautifully."

Shankar, even in 1997, was still amazed at the throng who applauded George Harrison and friends.

"It was a young audience, especially because I had this existing audience already, who were mature listeners and who had come to Carnegie Hall. This audience was the same type of audience as the Monterey Pop Festival, but they were very attentive and there was no problem at all. After our segment, I went to see the second half. Their program was very complementary, because they chose the numbers that were very soulful in the sense that they weren't hard rock. 'My Sweet Lord,' 'That's the Way God Planned It.' Bob Dylan had his harmonica and did ballads. George sang 'Here Comes the Sun' and the song he composed, 'Bangla Desh.' There was harmony and it wasn't so different. It went off beautifully. The soundtrack won a Grammy."

"Really, it was Ravi Shankar's idea," answered Harrison in a press conference held in New York in July 1971. "He wanted to do something like this and was telling me about his concern and asking me if I had any suggestions. Then after an hour he talked me into being on the show. It was a question really of phoning the friends that I knew and seeing who was available to turn up. I spent one month, the month of June and half of July, just telephoning people."

Pattie Boyd, former *Vogue* model, wife of George Harrison, inspiration for his "Something" and Eric Clapton's "Layla," had witnessed her husband organizing the Bangla Desh talent in the Nichols Canyon house they rented in Southern California for the summer of 1971.

"Pisces Apple Lady" Chris O'Dell also helped fellow Pisces George contact a few of the musicians for the undertaking.

"The first line of thinking from George was, 'Ravi has asked me to do something for him,'" O'Dell said to me in a July 2011 interview. "That's about friendship. That was more important than where it was gonna go. Even in the lyric to the song 'Miss O'Dell,' George had a reference to rice never making it to Bombay.

"George had told me about that situation earlier that summer. George was learning a lot from Ravi as time went by. So the idea of a concert didn't come up right off the bat. It came up later. Then it was, 'Would you help me?'

"And it was little things. Don Nix came into town. George didn't know him. We all went to Catalina Island together. I knew him from Leon. From that came the background singers.

"I don't think we had any idea of what it could be. I mean, it was fairly apparent that if you put a Beatle on stage, with a successful album behind him, *All Things Must Pass*, that it would probably draw people especially. John & Yoko did their things, but George hadn't, and you make an assumption that with George involved it's gonna draw people.

"George said, 'I can't believe this is all coming together.' The whole thing just grew right before our eyes."

Chris O'Dell also remembers Harrison's own mission in securing Bob Dylan for the gathering.

"That was part of the territory with him for a long time. And, you know, honestly, if George had an idol musically, that was it. So I think just having that piece there. George looked up to Bob in a way that there was that kind of esteem. And then the asking him to do something like that, and not wanting to let him down. George was really frightened by all this."

It was well documented that George and Pattie had concerns about Bob Dylan showing up at the Bangla Desh date. She was immediately relieved when Dylan actually showed up at the rehearsal.

O'Dell and Boyd were subsequently backstage for all the action and caught the second show in second-row center-stage seats.

At his music seminar at the Ash Grove music club in West Hollywood in 1971, Phil Spector rendered his Bob Dylan Bangla Desh story to the adoring throng.

"Nobody really knew Bob Dylan was coming, including us, 'cause he was out bicycle riding most of the morning. The funniest thing, we were all sitting in the hotel room and George said, 'Bob, do you think…it would really be groovy if you'd just come out one time and do a bit of 'Blowin' in the Wind?' Just turn them all on, you know.' 'Ummm, man, you gonna do 'I Want to Hold Your Hand?'"

In a 1971 radio interview on Los Angeles AM radio station KDAY, Spector previewed selections from his first-generation *Bangla Desh* master tape acetate.

Phil and the DJ aired Dylan's "A Hard Rain's A-Gonna Fall" from the concert as well as his non-released "Love

**Bob Dylan, Concert for Bangla Desh, August 1st, 1971
photo by Henry Diltz**

Minus Zero/No Limit," left off the original package due to vinyl space limitations of the period.

"Bob just came in right from bicycle riding on the day of the show. Bob just got up there and sang. It was probably the best performance he's ever done. In my opinion the album is worth buying just for Bob Dylan. And I'm not just trying to sell the album, but it's such an extraordinary performance."

Drummer Jim Keltner, who had worked with Spector on several John Lennon sessions, double-drummed with Ringo Starr at those charity shows for Bangla Desh relief.

Delaney & Bonnie & Friends' 1969 debut LP, *Accept No Substitute*, had made a musical impression on both George Harrison and Eric Clapton. Elektra Records A&R man David Anderle checked out Delaney & Bonnie's outfit gigging in a West L.A. club and brought them to the label to supervise their first LP, produced by Delaney Bramlett.

Billy Mundi and Jeff Simmons, during their Frank Zappa and Mothers of Invention employ, auditioned for the band, as did Duane Allman.

George Harrison had tried to sign Delaney & Bonnie to Apple Records in the U.K. after he had heard an early mix-down of their master tapes. Keltner even saw a Delaney & Bonnie acetate pressing with an Apple Records logo. However, the duo had a binding contract in place already with Jac Holzman's prestigious Elektra label.

"Leon [Russell] is all over that," reiterated Keltner. "His piano playing on 'The Ghetto' is the greatest. No one else can do that. When I got to know John [Lennon] he told me he liked the Delaney & Bonnie and Friends' *Accept No Substitute* album. I believe George turned John on to the record.

"After the earthquake in February of 1971 in Los Angeles, I told my wife, 'Get the kids together and get on over here.' We were there at a flat in Chelsea for a couple of months. During that time, George introduced me to Ringo and I played maracas on the single he produced for Ringo Starr at Trident Studio, 'It Don't Come Easy.'

"In 1971 we recorded the 'Bangla Desh' single with George Harrison and Phil Spector at Wally Heider's Studio 4 in Hollywood," Keltner reflected.

"So, when they asked me, I said, 'Of course, but I want to stay out of his way.' I didn't want to destroy anything of that great feel or his sound. When we actually sat down to play at the sound check, I had to decide on a few things. And one of the first decisions I made was to not play the hi-hat much. So I played the hi-hat like I had seen Levon [Helm] of the Band do, which was to pull the hand off the hi-hat for the two and four, so that it didn't come down with the back beat at the same time. And that helped me stay out of Ringo's way.

"But years later the cameraman told me, 'You really caused me some problems when I was editing that film, because your hand coming up like that I could never tell whether I was on the cut.'

"In fact, one night at Record Plant, somebody asked John, did he see the *Bangla Desh* film? John said he went to the premiere, and when he saw my face on the screen for the first time, he stood up and yelled, 'Hey—that's me drummer!' I fell on the floor."

"I remember loving the sound of the Garden," Keltner told me in a 2002 interview published in *Goldmine* magazine. "I heard Phil's voice over the speakers, but never really saw him at the actual show, except during sound check. He was in the Record Plant [recording] truck.

"Phil had his hands full and did a remarkable job if you really think about it. Horns, multiple singers, double drums, lots of guitars. That was his forte, so he wasn't intimidated by two drummers and 14 background singers. On *Bangla Desh*, George was very lucky to have had Phil on that set."

In my book *This Is Rebel Music*, Keltner said, "George was absolutely focused and fantastic as a leader. Of course he had Leon [Russell] in his band. And Leon helped with the arranging and all. I remember that everything seemed to be fine at the sound check and that I didn't have too many concerns. When we started playing with the audience in the room it really did come alive. George seemed very powerful that night.

"Ringo was a little on edge," Jim disclosed to me in an interview one evening at his home. The results were published in *Goldmine* in 2004. "He didn't fancy playing alone and was kinda unsure about his playing.

**George Harrison, Concert for Bangla Desh, August 1st 1971
photo by Henry Diltz**

"Playing on *Bangla Desh* was a really big deal for me. I made sure to stay completely out of Ringo's way and just played the bare minimum.

"Which is amazing if you think about it. One of rock's all-time great drummers. All you have to do is listen to the

Beatles records, of course, especially the *Live at the BBC*. Rock 'n' roll drumming doesn't get any better than that. Earl Palmer, Hal Blaine, Gary Chester, Fred Below, David 'Panama' Francis, great early rock and R&B drummers, and Ringo fit right in there with those guys. Listen to the BBC tapes and you'll hear what I'm saying."

**Ringo Starr, Concert for Bangla Desh August 1, 1971
photo by Henry Diltz**

On October 3, 2005, at the Steven J. Ross Theater in Burbank, California, on the Warner Bros. film lot, a gala was held to celebrate the 2005 CD/DVD launch of *The Concert for Bangladesh*.

I was invited to this function by Linda Arias, Olivia Harrison's sister, and directed to enter on the red carpet with Ringo Starr, Jim Keltner and John Densmore. My dream walking meditation drum jam session. This was not an just an earthly arrival. It was more like a metaphysical grounding. We then all sat together in the same row and viewed the film. Once in a while this is how I like to roll.

At the reception, a Concert for Bangladesh veterans' band with friends then performed, including Billy Preston on vocals and keyboards, drummers Ringo Starr and Jim Keltner, bassist Klaus Voormann, and Jim Horn and Chuck Findley of the Hollywood Horns.

It all reminded me of the press conference in Beverly Hills at the Beverly Wilshire Hotel when George Harrison was promoting his U.S. solo tour. My notes from that event were printed in the November 2, 1974, issue of *Melody Maker.*

On meeting the Beatles, Harrison reflected, "Biggest break in my career was getting into the Beatles. In retrospect, biggest break since then was getting out of them."

Was he ever amazed about how much the Beatles still mean to people?

"Not really. I mean, it's nice. I realize the Beatles did fill a space in the Sixties. All the people the Beatles meant something to have grown up. It's like anything you grow up with—you get attached to things.

"I understand the Beatles in many ways did nice things, and it's appreciated that people still like them. They want to hold on to something. People are afraid of change. You can't live in the past."

George Harrison was asked about the role of the entertainer in working with causes and charities.

"I don't think it's an entertainer's job. He does what he can. And I do it through music. It's not isolated to musicians."

In his '74 interaction with global media, Harrison itemized the charities he would be working with on his tour that year, including "a concert in Los Angeles for the Self Realization Fellowship. It was founded by Paramahansa Yogananda. He happened to be a big influence in my life. I'd like to repay his in a small way."

"George Harrison's Bangla Desh concert presented Ravi Shankar, who is holy man spiritual inspiration for George's ethereal escapades and adventures," concludes musical historian Kim Fowley.

"As the Bangla Desh shows and the CD/DVD product and re-releases hit age 40, it's like fine wine in a billionaire's wine cellar who brings it up for the important guests. It's the vintage element. In an instant-information era which is not flavor of the month anymore. It's flavor of the moment; I just coined it. Flavor of the moment, there's no fiber of backup. It's, 'Oh. Here's something new, bright, nice and noisy.' Now it's gone for the next thing that is bright, shiny and noisy. And only in the past in pop culture do you go to something that has lasted forever. It is the European vantage point of old.

"Bangla Desh is now appreciated because it stood the test of time. As opposed to the latest phenomena on YouTube or Facebook that will be forgotten by dinnertime. And that's why it's good—because it is based on tradition, and tradition is something the new cycle is missing. And that's why it's worth checking out. If you were young and weren't there the first time, you get to see where it all comes from, and it has a richness and depth of culture. And secondly, if you were there, it reminds you how much better things were yesterday. Because tomorrow is fast-food entertainment.

"When the Beatles started hanging out in Hollywood and Los Angeles with David Crosby, Peter Fonda, and the Benedict Canyon type of people," elaborated Fowley in 2011, "George went a little further and began wishing he was in a band like Delaney & Bonnie & Friends, who became the blueprint and the template for the Concert for Bangla Desh. Leon Russell, Carl Radle, Jim Keltner and Eric Clapton. Eric was more American emotionally than he ever was English.

"George was the most American of all the Beatles. He had been to America and St. Louis before the band came to New York in 1964. George Harrison wrote 'Blue Jay Way,' so he was the first Beatle to write a song about America."

Dr. James Cushing examines The Concert for Bangla Desh.

"It might have been the first time in history that a major rock concert begins with the star asking the audience to settle down instead of saying, 'Let's party.' And then, he hits them with music from an ancient Indian tradition by two of its greatest virtuosos.

"Is George Harrison India's greatest cultural ambassador? In my experience, many Americans, unless they've actually met an Indian person, primarily associate Indian culture with what George Harrison first exposed them to: 'Norwegian Wood' and 'Within You Without You.' Sometimes I think George Harrison is one of the reasons Indian cuisine caught on in the United States.

"Musically, in terms of sheer degree of artistry, Ravi Shankar and Ali Akbar Khan's 'Bangla Dhun' is the high point of the *Bangla Desh* album. I felt that way in 1972 and I feel the same way now. Shankar and Khan become invocations of India, and this benefit concert at one level must be about India. Of course, on another level, Ringo singing 'It Don't Come Easy' and Dylan singing 'Mr. Tambourine Man' and George doing 'Something' have nothing at all to do with India. But the concert does! So how do you assemble a concert of non-Indian music and make it relevant to India? There is only one way: put some authentic Indian masters on the bill.

"Harrison seems aware that the 'old world' of India has an ambivalent place in the 'new world' of rock: This music is 'a bit more serious than our music,' he explains to the crowd.

We respect Harrison's humility here; he and his all-star band couldn't do what these masters do. Devoted to Indian music, he gives his guests the star turn.

"There is an extremely sincere devotional element in almost all Harrison's songwriting and performances, and it gives his work a certain power, focus and respectability. But the other side of that element is a didactic tendency to preach. Beware of darkness, isn't it a pity, you must learn the art of dying: lo and behold, here comes George Harrison to save humanity from the darkness by telling us what we need to do.

"At the same time, I hear caution and fragility in George's singing at the Bangla Desh concert, an unusually interior kind of voice for Madison Square Garden. We can tell he's nervous about the way this show is going to go when he forgets to introduce Billy Preston.

"But Preston, too, connects with Harrison's devotional aesthetic. This white East Coast audience gets both a taste of India and a taste of Watts with 'That's the Way God Planned It.' Preston was an authentic master of the gospel idiom and willing to find ways to work that idiom into secular music, just as he did when George invited him on the 'Get Back' recording sessions.

"Leon Russell knew that sound too. At the concert, 'Beware of Darkness,' with Russell singing one verse and Jim Horn playing sax, became more of a blessing than a warning. We hear an African-American gospel group with a British lead singer afloat on Hindu religious mythology. And this long-haired Oklahoma boy Leon drawls a country-western take on the whole verse. So, add Americana plus India, plus England, plus religious devotion, plus gospel, plus rock superstardom. Only in America. A masala!"

It Was 50 Years Ago Today: The Beatles Invade America and Hollywood

Steve Van Zandt May, 2011, Lillehammer, Norway

"The anti-apartheid Sun City project (single, album, video, documentary, book, teaching guide) was a high point and a rare clear-cut victory from the 10 years I spent immersed in the dark, murky, frustrating labyrinth of international liberation politics.

"It came in the middle of my five politically themed solo albums and had its roots, like all the charity and consciousness-raising multi-artist events that would follow, in the Concert for Bangladesh.

"One could go back seven years further to the work of Bob Dylan for the reason my generation had any political or social awareness at all. He would single-handedly bring the more personal, socially, and politically relevant lyrics previously confined to country blues, country, and folk music to the pop and rock idiom. The fact that he probably did so to impress his girlfriend Suze at the time, rather than some grand megalomaniacal scheme to become the spokesperson of his generation, just makes him all the more human and likable and is probably the reason he's still around and still great.

"And it's not a coincidence that he's the one artist on both *Bangladesh* and 'Sun City' 15 years later.

"But it was the Concert for Bangladesh that would be the beginning of all the multi-artist events bringing awareness to a cause and/or raising money.

"It would take the energy and focus of a Beatle, George Harrison, to bring the extraordinary necessary life force to get the event organized and executed so quickly and with such high quality.

"The unfortunate financial complications that followed was the one thing that couldn't be foreseen by noble naïve artists trying to do the right thing in an emergency situation.

Part 4: Save the Tiger

The despicable, mindless, emotionless bureaucracy they would run into would later instruct all of us who followed.

"But that aside, it was a wonderful event and we all owe George our gratitude. All of us who have ever had the desire to use—and justify—our celebrity to do some good, as well as the tens of millions who have benefited from these events, all have him to thank. Him, and the generous heart of the legendary master musician Ravi Shankar, who came to his friend with the desire to bring aid and attention to a terrible, tragic situation.

"As far as history is concerned, we shouldn't take for granted the fact that these charity and awareness events exist, and that the rock world has done more than any other industry to help people in need. This was not some inevitable act of destiny or even a predictable evolution of what turned out to be a 25-year successful run of the music business.

"The idea had to start somewhere. The source is the Concert for Bangladesh."

The Rock and Roll Forever Foundation (RRFF; http://www.rockandrollforever.org) has been set up by Steven Van Zandt to provide a curriculum initiative for U.S. schools.

RRFF has created Rock and Roll: An American Story (RRAS) as a course designed for middle and high schools in the U.S., which will be provided free of cost to interested schools.

In 2013, an article I wrote in 2011, "With a Little Help from His Friends: George Harrison and the Concert for Bangladesh," first published in *RECORD COLLECTOR news* and then *Rock's Backpages*, was chosen by RRFF for the curriculum. This will be a 40-chapter history of rock 'n' roll. Each chapter will have three to six individual lesson plans associated with it along with visual and audio materials.

The last time I physically saw George Harrison was in 1998 one cosmic afternoon in the house of a mutual musician friend in Los Angeles.

When I arrived, Harrison warmly greeted me with, "Well, at least here you don't have to take your shoes off like at Ravi's house!" He was reviewing tapes in the home studio on the premises. George and I share our February 26th birthday with Fats Domino, Sandie Shaw, and Johnny Cash.

George had seen spoken-word artist Eddie Izzard's show at the Tiffany Theater in West Hollywood and offered a good recommendation of a local Indian restaurant in West Hollywood he frequented, Taste of India. He had just dined there with his wife Olivia and Jim Capaldi. When we parted I gave him some freeway directions to his in-laws in the South Bay area.

Ravi Shankar published his autobiography *Raga Mala* in September 2001; it was edited and introduced by George Harrison.

Over the last few decades, Harrison and Shankar would, on occasion, visit Self-Realization Fellowship in Encinitas, California, the beach community near San Diego where Shankar lived with his second wife Sukanya from 1992 on.

The windmill chapel at the Lake Shrine in Pacific Palisades, California, carries on Paramahansa Yogananda's spiritual and humanitarian Self-Realization Fellowship work and legacy and hosted George Harrison's funeral service in 2001.

In 1973 my family lived in West Hollywood, less than a mile away from Blue Jay Way. The internal photo of George Harrison's 1973 *Living in the Material World* LP was taken at a Doheny estate just around the corner from our house.

Rock 'n' Roll was the sixth studio album by John Lennon, and it began in Los Angeles in October 1973 at A&M Studios on La Brea Avenue.

Keyboardist/arranger Don Randi, a Spector studio group veteran since 1962, was on the L.A. sessions. Four of the tracks would be added to the New York City Lennon recordings done at Record Plant for the official album release in 1975.

"There were always great songs," testifies Randi about re-cutting versions of oldies but goodies, the chosen Lennon and Spector favorites for a re-do LP. "The songs always told a story. The songs in themselves were films. And, especially in Phil's case, he knew how to write them and how to produce them.

"Most of the times when we did those studio jobs we were asked to be somebody else. We were cloned. You know, if somebody wanted Floyd Cramer you had to come out. If somebody wanted a more Ray Charles sound you had to come up with it. If somebody wanted more of a Phil Spector sound then I knew exactly what they wanted."

Dan Kessel is an acclaimed multi-instrumentalist and record producer. In 2011 and 2013 Dan emailed me with some reflections and comments about working with Phil Spector and John Lennon and meeting John and George in Hollywood, as well as providing background stories about his father—jazz icon, session great, record producer and former Verve Records A&R man Barney Kessel—and the 12-string guitar.

"On some of the early Crystals records with Phil Spector, my dad used a Guild acoustic 12-string that he commissioned to be modified by repairman Milt Owen by adding a pickup so it could also be played as an electric. Incidentally, a few years later, my dad would enlist Milt to be the house luthier and repairman at Barney Kessel's Music World in Hollywood, near Du-par's and the Capitol Records building. My dad's early electrified acoustic Guild 12-string got a unique and substantially different sound than what was to come with the Rickenbacker 12-string, which wasn't out yet, or by the time of the later records had only just come out.

"Some of the Ric's characteristic jangly sound is produced in part by the unique sound chamber of its body style in combination with thinner-gauge strings and low-output toaster pickups. Of course, Harrison, Townshend and others made great use of this new guitar and then McGuinn took the sound to another level with his unique style and special combination of compression, delay and treble boost.

"While I was recording with John Lennon in the '70s, he mentioned that my dad's 12-string riff on 'Then He Kissed Me' was an inspiration for the Beatles' getting into the Rickenbacker 12 on their records, which kind of blew my mind. John laughed, though, when I told him that my dad had switched from that Guild to the Rickenbacker 12-string for record dates in '65 after the Beatles and Byrds had firmly established that sound. John said it was ironic and he was intrigued at how Barney influenced them but how it all went back around again and how everybody influences each other.

"My stepbrother [actor Tim Rooney] and stepmother [singer B.J. Baker] and brother David and I ran into George Harrison during a party at film director Richard Quine's home in the Hollywood Hills. Tim was dating Quine's daughter, Casey. Some of the other guests included people like Fred Astaire, Count Basie and Kim Novak. George loved the house and expressed his interest in buying if Quine ever wanted to sell. Mr. Astaire had some complimentary dialogue with me about my dad, whom he admired. They had worked together recording a couple of Astaire's albums. George, who'd been

Part 4: Save the Tiger

hovering nearby, joined the conversation, giving compliments to Mr. Astaire and offering me compliments about my dad. He expressed that he'd been wanting to meet him for quite some time. Phil Spector had tried to introduce them once before but my dad bailed because he had an early-morning cartoon date and those scores were harder to read than Stravinsky. But that night, I offered to arrange it for George.

"My dad was at home visiting with his friend, Jimmy Wyble, guitarist with Bob Wills & the Texas Playboys. A Texan and contemporary of my dad's, they'd become friends early on and had gone to each other's gigs in Texas and in Oklahoma, where my dad was born and raised before going on the road with big bands as a teen and settling into L.A.'s Laurel Canyon in the late '40s. Tim, B.J. and I brought Harrison over to meet my dad and Jimmy Wyble. George was very nice and complimentary and a bit humble actually in the company of the older jazz guys, who both took to him very well. He knew just enough about western swing (a distant cousin to jazz/rockabilly) to be conversant, and he acquitted himself nicely when he took a stab at joining them in playing 'San Antonio Rose.' The three guitarists, some of the best in their genres, got along well and had a good time together.

"Phil Spector asked me to play guitar on the *Rock 'n' Roll* album that he was doing with John Lennon. My brother David and I worked on that with them.

"After playing on those recordings we were excited about becoming part of the Wrecking Crew. We then joined the Musicians Union and continued recording on more major sessions with Spector and others. Concurrently, we got very involved with the beginnings of the early L.A. punk scene and recorded with N.Y. bands like the Ramones and Blondie.

"We'd met John Lennon on a couple of occasions as kids, including back in late '66 and early '67 in London with Jimi Hendrix, Brian Jones, and lots of people like that," Kessel offered. "And we ran into John again, as well as George Harrison and the Byrds, at Barney Kessel's Music World in Hollywood.

"Throughout the *Rock 'n' Roll* recording sessions, I'd talk to John whenever feasible during breaks and between takes. He actually fell in deep love with my customized Gibson Everly Brothers guitar, so I let him use it during some of the sessions. In fact, I told him afterward that I'd be honored for him to keep it. He accepted on the condition that I accept his guitar, which I gladly did."

Dan and John Lennon had some memorable time together at the wet and wild Spector and Lennon dates, occurring around John Lennon's 18-month "Lost Weekend" in Hollywood.

"John and I were easily able to agree that 'Angel Baby' by Rosie and the Originals was one of the greatest records all time, for many different reasons, which we discussed at great length. And, after drinking quite a bit, we got all excited and emotional, crying tears about it and the genius of the B-side, 'Give Me Love,' and about how we wished we could have been in the Originals. John was eager to hear anything I had to say about Rosie and the Originals and Julian Hererra and guys like Little Ray and Little Willie G. and stories I told him about Ritchie Valens and the El Monte Legion Stadium.

"I can still see John smiling, talking with my friend Blake Xolton, a musician who was helping me out as my equipment tech. They discussed the L.A. T-Birds roller derby team of the '60s and some of their key players like Ralphie Valladares, Danny Reilly, Judy Sowinski, Toni Tagg. John remembered watching them on TV when in L.A. as a Beatle.

"But then, after an especially intense take…John, and my brother and I with Blake Xolton and Hal Blaine, Nino Tempo, Don Peake, and some of the others are summoned by Phil over the talk-back speaker to come into the control booth. With dimmed lights, Phil plays back a rough mix of 'Angel Baby' at full volume. The speakers try not to explode, while suddenly the booth is transformed into a séance, with all kinds of ghosts, sonic and otherwise, swirling out of the speakers, surrounding the booth and encircling the studio. Dumbstruck, in awe, we shudder at the sheer insane, unearthly magnificence. Suddenly John and all of us are trembling, crying, hugging, laughing… while Phil screams out at the top of his lungs that rock 'n' roll will never die!"

John Lennon spent time in Hollywood from 1973 through 1975. He would be at Schwab's Pharmacy on Sunset Boulevard and would eat at the famed lunch counter and read the paper without being disturbed.

"In late 1973 I was managing Doug Weston's Troubadour in West Hollywood," offers Robert Marchese. "John Lennon came in with Elton John. They ended up jamming one night with Dr. John and Bobby Womack. John spent some time in the area and used to frequent Valdez Guitar Shop which is on Sunset Boulevard.

"In early 1974 Lennon was in the club again with May Pang to see Ann Peebles. He loved her record 'I Can't Stand the Rain.' Lennon had a Kotex stuck on his head. He might have been drinking. Lennon was lewd to Ann Peebles during her set, yelling out, 'Annie I wanna suck you!' My waitress said, 'It's a shame when your idols turn out to be assholes.'

"One night in in '74 Lennon arrived to the Troubadour with May Pang, Harry Nilsson and Peter Lawford. We put them in the raised area. John kept on heckling the Smothers Brothers who were onstage. Finally, Tommy Smothers over the microphone asked me to do something about this. The Troubadour went into complete silence.

"I lean over and put my hand on Lennon's wrist and my other hand on Nilsson's wrist. I had thrown out Nilsson one other time. They were drunk. I then said to Lennon, nose to nose, 'You know, in 1963 a guy got killed and the whole world went into a stage of depression. And then in '64 four guys from Liverpool came out and made everybody forget what happened in '63. Here you are sitting beside the brother-in-law of that guy. Don't you feel like a big fuckin' asshole?' And he replied, 'Yes I do.' 'Would you please leave?' And he got up and walked out.

"Apparently this had happened because John had broken up with Yoko. Lennon and Nilsson then had a drunken incident with the paparazzi behind the Troubadour alley.

"The next day, John later sent a wonderful apology note and lots of flowers and candies to the Smothers Brothers that filled their dressing room. There was a reference to me in the note, 'to thank the gentleman in the football jersey who handled a very bad situation well.' Lennon also left his glasses at the Troubadour and we returned them."

Lennon and I chatted during 1974 inside the former Santa Monica home of Peter Lawford one night at the record playback party for the Harry Nilsson *Pussy Cats* album John produced. Ringo was in attendance. Nancy Rose Retchin and I had a card game with Ringo and Harry for two hours.

Later in the year, several music reporters were invited to follow and tape Lennon's promotional radio tour coinciding with his just-released *Walls and Bridges* solo album around his KHJ stop on Melrose Avenue.

During that September 27, 1974, radio interview on KHJ, where he played DJ for an hour on Superstars Week, Lennon spun the Wailers' "Get Up, Stand Up" and sang a lyric line from Ritchie Valens' "Donna" to a stunned phone caller named Donna.

Lennon was sitting in for jock Charlie Van Dyke. John spun all-time favorite records of local heroes like Gene Vincent's "Be-Bop-a-Lula" and Little Richard's "Long Tall Sally."

John slotted his own "Instant Karma" and "Beef Jerky" compositions. "I think it's the first instrumental I've done and the Beatles did very few," he noted of the latter. "It's 7:19 in this part of the world. The rest of the world, I don't know what time it is."

A listener named Lance from Canoga Park requested "It's Only Love" from *Rubber Soul* and Lennon responded, "The only song I ever did I didn't like. All right! We might play it. I'll have to suffer. Hello KHJ. This is Fred Astaire here. What's cookin'?"

Lennon even provided numerous weather reports. "It's 64 in Hollywood now. Believe it or not. It's 8:05 in Southern California. I'm John Lennon still." When someone asked about concerts, Lennon responded, "Concerts? I probably will someday. But at the moment I don't really feel like runnin' all over the place. Let me do a radio spot here for Tower Records in the heart of Sunset Strip."

Lennon read commercial copy for Orange County International Raceways, and then tracked "Jet" by Wings. "KHJ. That was Paul. Wasn't that a good one? That was one of his goodies. I wanted to play 'Monkberry Moon Delight' but it was too long."

Lennon put "My Sweet Lord" in rotation. "That was a great one from George. He'll be touring soon on a Dark Horse." After spinning his own "Going Down on Love," John was questioned about his black Rickenbacker. "I still have my black Rickenbacker, which used to be a blonde Rickenbacker, which is the first good guitar I ever had. Yes I do have it."

His visit closed with a pre-existing taped Ringo radio spot for *Walls and Bridges* and then segueing into "Whatever Gets You Through the Night."

"This is John Lennon on KHJ. And I'm just saying goodbye now. I had a great time. I hope you did. I'd like to thank the people at KHJ."

Yoko Ono, John Lennon and Ringo Starr, May, 1976, West Hollywood. Rainbow Bar & Grill photo by Brad Elterman.

In May 1976, I talked to John Lennon again just after he, Yoko Ono and I watched an awe-inspiring Bob Marley & the Wailers visitation at the Roxy Theatre. The Wailers had covered "And I Love Her" with producer Coxson Dodd in 1965. I thanked John for introducing me to reggae, ska and blue beat music that he would reference during interviews. With Tom Donahue on KSAN-FM in 1974 he talked about the Wailers. John knew my weekly Los Angeles column from *Melody Maker*.

I mentioned his 1974 KHJ DJ guest stint and the Wailers' "Get Up, Stand Up" airplay on his shift. I was with Rick Nielsen of Cheap Trick, with whom he would later record. We walked over to the Rainbow Bar & Grill next door, where he and Yoko were joining Ringo.

In 1976 or '77 I was introduced to George Martin at the opening of the Chrysalis Records office in West Hollywood on Sunset Boulevard. We didn't talk about the Beatles. Mr. Martin spoke about his production of Jeff Beck's *Blow by Blow* at the reception.

Near the end of the last century I had another conversation with Sir George Martin after he had faxed me on his letterhead an encouraging note lauding my production of a Ray Manzarek spoken-word album.

We met at the Hollywood Bowl the next time he was in Los Angeles when his office invited me to Martin's sound check for a program he was conducing and narrating of Beatles songs. "The group did a lot of quality material," he quipped around a rehearsal break that sunny afternoon.

A few years ago, I connected again with Martin and his son Giles at the landmark Capitol Records building inside their renowned Studio B. It was a media gathering and playback unveiling for the Beatles' *LOVE* album that day.

LOVE, the latest Cirque du Soleil creation, a co-production with Apple Corps Ltd., celebrates and respects the musical legacy of the Beatles and is presented exclusively at the Mirage in Las Vegas.

The *LOVE* project was born out of a personal friendship and mutual admiration between the George Harrison and Cirque du Soleil founder Guy Laliberté.

As music director for *LOVE*, Giles Martin is at the epicenter of a revolution in the musical legacy of the Beatles while working side by side with his father, Sir George Martin.

"Our first mission was to try and achieve the same intimacy we get when listening to the master tapes at Abbey Road Studios," Giles stressed to me in a telephone interview for *WAVES!* "The last thing we wanted to create was a retrospective or a tribute show. The Beatles, above all else, were a great rock band. With the manipulation of the tracks and the huge number of speakers in the theater, the audience will feel as though they are actually in the room with the boys.

"All the Beatles were very encouraging. After the initial demo thing, they made me feel part of the process. With both Ringo and Paul, my main memory, my biggest, fondest moment of the whole thing, was nothing to do with me: both Paul and Ringo said to me that I had been so sensitive with our material and really taken it in, and that means a great deal, but the thing that struck me was at Abbey Road was listening to 'Come Together' with them both and individually. They weren't together at the time. 'God, we were really good on this day. I remember this day. We really nailed this.'

"For them to appreciate their own craft, without any of the politics, or any of the hyperbole, or the other stuff that goes on, it's four guys in the room listening by two mates themselves, and really just remembering what a great time they had.

"A lot of people listen to the Beatles in a conventional way—radio, iPod or car, for example—but never in such a space. I think we have achieved a real sense of drama with the music in the theater," stated Giles.

"We wanted to make sure there are enough good, solid hit songs in the show, but we don't want it to be a catalog of 'best ofs,'" reinforced Sir George Martin. "We also wanted to put in some interesting and not well-known Beatles music and use fragments of songs. The show is a unique and magical experience."

"George and Giles did such a great job combining these tracks. It's really powerful for me and I even heard things I'd forgotten we'd recorded," remarked Ringo Starr.

"This album puts the Beatles back together again, because suddenly there's John and George with me and Ringo," tenders Paul McCartney. "It's kind of magical."

In the Capitol facility, Sir George and I talked briefly about a Frank Sinatra recording session he had attended in this very same room on his first visit to Hollywood, in 1958. The EMI label sent him over the pond after Martin was invited by Capitol executive Voyle Gilmore to visit the American division.

Martin described that date when Sinatra was backed by Billy May's orchestra while actress Lauren Bacall was in attendance. The songs cut were eventually placed on Sinatra's *Come Fly With Me* LP.

I wanted to make it a point to personally thank George Martin for discovering and signing the Beatles to their British record label deal in the first place. And to praise his persistent determination, along with Brian Epstein, in prodding Capitol Records U.S. company to have some faith in Martin's groundbreaking Parlophone/EMI recordings with the band back in 1963.

It was at my most recent Martin encounter, where one of his Beatles productions started playing in Studio B. Try hearing their music over custom TAD monitors.

George then autographed a solo album, put his arm around me and observed, "Pretty good stuff. Don't you think?"

In 2013 I said to Ken Scott that the one thing that astonishes me about the 50-year recording career of the Beatles on the EMI label is that all this early work—well, at least in 1963—was done without advocates, label support, and only faint music publishing interest from inception, under such skepticism and lack of any faith in the lads.

"You've got this band that comes in. They have a moderate amount of success with a single which contains two of their songs and they're signed to the EMI publishing company Ardmore Beechwood. They are going to do a second single and the publishing company is asked, 'So, do you want to sign them for publishing on the next single?' And they turned them down. A complete lack of belief. The way I heard it—this is memory, and second- or third-hand—my understanding was that George [Martin] had to persuade Dick James to even sign them for publishing.

"George knew Dick from a 1956 single of 'Robin Hood' he cut with him that Dick sang. Then he got into publishing. When George approached Dick about working with the Beatles, the way I heard it, Dick was at that moment even considering leaving the publishing business. George said to him, 'Look, I've got this band and Ardmore Beechwood has passed. Why don't you sign them?' 'Oh, I don't know…' 'Look, what have you got to lose? We're going to do a single. Sign them and see what happens.' And the rest is history. So there was a total lack of belief in anything that they were doing in the beginning.

"I just received an award from him. The Sound Fellowship of the United Kingdom's Association of Professional Recording Services (APRS). The man who first kicked me out of the control room at age 16. Absolutely astounding moment.

"Walking in his footsteps to a point and realizing. I think it first started to change when I heard David [Bowie] had called me 'his George Martin' on the BBC in England. And my first thing was, 'I don't know if I like that.' Then when I started to think through it I realized how much I had taken from George and just that whole thing of allowing the artistic freedom. And you're there to give advice. To control if you have to, but don't overdo that control.

"Artists need to create. And that's what you have to let them do. Creating is just like breathing for them. You can't stop them breathing. And I got that from George. I was young and learning my gig, so that didn't quite resonate with me the way it does today."

I asked Scott in 2013 if he had any ideas on why he and I were still talking about the Beatles' catalogue, 50 years on?

"Because of the changes going on in that period of time, their music and they have become more important. They were very much a part of the major change within the Western civilization. A lot of it stemming from the Second World War. Because of the baby boom. Younger people were getting more of a say. More power. And that helped to change things, which they were a major part of.

"I also feel that a lot of it is because it's real. They were performances. It's not like it is today, where it's all pieced together. Yes, we would do punch-ins and that kind of thing, but there wasn't copying one chorus and putting it in every chorus so it's always exactly the same. They had to sing and play everything. And they had this ability, which so few other acts had—the closest I would probably come is U2— but they had this ability of being able to take the audience, their audience, through changes. Without losing them. They always moved just enough that they could pull their audience with them and have the audience grow along with them."

Ken Scott has also heard his work with the Beatles on vinyl, eight-track cartridges, tape cassettes, compact discs and the digital universe.

"To me it's analog vinyl to CD. I find digital quite often cold compared to analog. There's a warmth and a depth, if you like, to analog, be it vinyl, be it tape, that we don't get in the digital domain. We will eventually, but we're not quite there yet. The whole point for me was that we had to move away from vinyl, at least for pop music, because the vinyl that was being used for albums was becoming so bad and so noisy that records were becoming thinner and thinner. It had to change. The way we listen to music had to change. And CDs, even as bad as they were, when they first came out, were better than the quality of the vinyl at that point. I think now there's probably more—the availability of vinyl has improved, so the vinyl being used for the records is at a higher standard."

"Now we're not just going into a record store for a new Beatles' experience but the new Beatles' album," asserts Dr. James Cushing. "The last time you could really say that was 1970. The excitement of being able to get something new from the Beatles is the excitement of being able to have a temporary victory over time. It can be 1970 again.

"In general, the meaning of their music keeps on changing, of course. With the death of Michael Jackson the Beatles are now in an era that is previous to the era that has now ended. So they've become kind of more and more distant in history and hence more and more mythic."

The Beatles' *On Air—Live at the BBC Volume 2* was released on Monday, November 11, 2013, in 2-CD and 180-gram-vinyl packages with a 48-page booklet. *On Air's* 63 tracks, none of which overlaps with the *Live at the BBC 1994* double album (which was also also remastered and reissued simultaneously), includes 37 previously unreleased performances and 23 previously unreleased recordings of in-studio banter and conversation between the band members and their BBC radio hosts.

In the studios of the British Broadcasting Corporation, the Beatles performed music for a variety of radio shows. *On Air—Live at the BBC Volume 2* presents the sound of the Beatles seizing their moment to play for a devoted radio audience and a nation of listeners.

As John Lennon recalled in 1980 about the BBC's most important pop show of the early '60s, "We did a lot of tracks that were never on record for *Saturday Club*—they were well recorded, too." Paul remembers, "We'd been raised on the BBC radio programs. One of the big things in our week was *Saturday Club*—this great show was playing the kind of music we loved, so that was something we really aspired to."

Between March 1962 and June 1965, no fewer than 275 unique musical performances by the Beatles were broadcast by the BBC in the U.K. The group played songs on 39 radio shows in 1963 alone. Ringo Starr said in 1994, "You tend to forget that we were a working band. It's that mono sound. There were usually no overdubs. We were in at the count-in and that was it. I get excited listening to them."

The Beatles had to play live at the BBC. "Everything was done instantly," remembered George Harrison, "But before that, we used to drive 200 miles in an old van down the M1, come into London, try and find the BBC and then set up and do the program. Then we'd probably drive back to Newcastle for a gig in the evening!"

"Working for Universal Music Enterprises as Director Of Radio & Tour Promotion over the last decade, it was quite obvious to me that the Beatles' monumental back catalog and franchise was in great demand and that the group continues to retain great influence in the terrestrial and satellite radio world," reinforced Elliot Kendall.

"We serviced *The 4 Complete Ed Sullivan Shows Starring The Beatles* DVD package to Classic Rock and Classic Hits formats - in addition to Beatles specialty shows in the U.S. and in the Los Angeles market at stations KCSN, KLOS, and KRTH. I also promoted both *Y Not* and *2012* albums by Ringo Starr, in addition to promoting and setting up theatrical screenings for the Martin Scorsese-directed George Harrison *Living In The Material World* documentary.

"The Beatles Sullivan Show DVD remains a pivotal release. It continues to be the 'Big Bang' or 'Ground Zero' of the band's launch in this country. It's incredibly essential and compelling to re-examine it now, seeing all the other various acts that shared the stage at the time (including a young Davy Jones of The Monkees portraying the Artful Dodger). When The Beatles finally appear, their presentation is confident, complete and entirely revolutionary.

"When the band finally reached Los Angeles, naturally they were infatuated with Hollywood - but they kept their edge and their game face on, unimpressed by reporters asking inane questions or dignitaries making outrageous requests.

"Perhaps having been a product of working class Liverpool gave them an iron-clad work ethic and made them into indestructible music machines, determined to not only hold onto the hurricane of fame, but to harness it and utilize it on their own terms, breaking the then-existing mold and creating new templates at each and every turn.

"Bob Dylan has a great quote about how outrageous their chords were that The Beatles used in song construction. Early on, the band double-tracked their vocals (as did the Beach Boys and others) which gave the sound a pleasing if slightly phasing effect, essentially blending two riveting vocal performances into one powerful presentation. The bed tracks of their recordings were based on the raw energetic fire of their rock & roll heroes, Elvis, Little Richard, Eddie Cochran, Gene Vincent, Carl Perkins, Motown and more - somewhere within all these and other elements lie many of the Beatles' secrets for success," presents Kendall.

"Broadcasting will continue to go through many changes - but in my opinion, the power of personality and the presentation of compelling content will be the common thread of its attraction. The Beatles' music and power of pop culture is tailor made for this presentation - we all love a great story, and the band has countless tales, both musical and biographical. Much has been said about radio and its 'Theater Of The Mind' magic - may it long weave that spell and may we all long enjoy it."

"I heard one of my favorite podcast hosts, Marc Maron, saying that Beatles songs had become so ubiquitous that in some ways they had become like Christmas carols," conveyed record business executive Gary Stewart. "He meant this not in a derogatory way but as a reminder that people may forget to take a closer look at underplayed album cuts or make the real effort to find something new, scary, or revelatory in the established classics.

"The Christmas carol remark made me think also about why the Beatles are so endearing. The brilliant, effective and sometime deceptive simplicity of songs like 'She Loves You,' 'I Want to Hold Your Hand' and 'Yellow Submarine' hold sway over so many very young children today. I saw *Help!* when I was nine, *Yellow Submarine* when I was 12, and drove my parents crazy for both repeat viewings and soundtrack albums—a heavily replicated experienced with many of today's preteens. That their DNA and influence can always be found something (most things) on the Top 40 ever since then also explains that longevity.

"Less talked about is the role they play in the indie rock revolution now personified by Fader, Lollapalooza, Coachella, etc. It seems counterintuitive to think that the biggest seemingly mainstream artist in pop music history would have a connection with the likes of Radiohead and Arcade Fire, but listen with Coachella ears to tracks like 'Blue Jay Way,' 'Polythene Pam' and "Within You Without You' and it's not a big leap.

"The entirety of the *White Album*—not just for its content but for its variety and experimentation—influences most everything in this sector and would rightfully catch the gaze of Pitchfork.com were it released today.

"When I worked at iTunes and they launched the Beatles catalog, I remember how many contemporary artists participated in talking about their favorite Beatles songs," Stewart continued. "And when the catalog continued to make appearances in the upper reaches of the sales charts well beyond launch, how easy it was to forget the 40-year difference.

"More importantly," he deduced, "I hope people that do experience these things like Christmas carols will dig deeper and find strange nooks and crannies that reveal something new, and relate it to what they are listening to now, more than then."

"As a friend of mine said, 'New music is anything you haven't heard.' Surprising, but there really are new things by the Beatles you haven't heard (or really paid attention to)."

At a 2011 lecture at a University of Southern California Cinematic Arts lecture for Professor David James' class in the Critical Studies Division, after the question-and-answer session, a student asked about my three specific favorite moments of the Beatles onscreen.

I quickly rattled off four of them: *A Hard Day's Night,* with George fronting the band on "I'm Happy Just to Dance With You." The boys on *The David Frost Show* delivering "Hey Jude" to the universe. Another fab exposure was Cilla Black performing "It's For You" on *The Music of Lennon and McCartney*, a British TV special. Paul and John have a cameo after Cilla sings their tune. Maybe the best Beatles on videotape cartridge had to be a glued-in studio throng surrounding the foursome trading lead vocals on a sermon-like "Shout" documented on *Around the Beatles*.

During February 7-9th 2014, The Fest For Beatles Fans took place in New York City. Close associates of the Beatles -- Donovan, Peter Asher, Billy J. Kramer, Chad & Jeremy, Prudence Farrow, Larry Kane and the former UK head of the Beatles Fan Club, Freda Kelly who is profiled in the documentary *Good Ol' Freda* -- celebrated 50 years of the Beatles in America. The Fest began in 1974 as the brainchild of Mark Lapidos. In 2014 The Fest travels to Chicago during August and Los Angeles in October.

The Beatles' recordings are like souvenirs from a dream. The dream being the great romance of the 20th century. These four people captured the imaginations of the world and put so much positive energy into their imaginations—then turned the love and anxiety of the period into a lasting musical testimonial.

The JOHN LENNON SHIRTS

Small, Medium, Large

Available Now At

Beau Gentry

1523 North Vine

September 1965 newspaper ad courtesy Jim Roup

EPILOGUE:

"For kids that were born in the late '60s but grew up in the '70s, the Beatles had a special power by absence," theorizes writer Daniel Weizmann. "The entire '70s, for us, was colored by their breakup, even as glitter, disco, punk, and society-at-large raged forward.

"On *Saturday Night Live,* Lorne Michaels joked about staging a reunion, but really, you knew it wouldn't happen—you'd been cheated out of some lost utopia that no *Kids Are Alright* documentary, no *Goat's Head Soup* was gonna recreate.

"At a Beatles convention at the Hollywood Palladium on Sunset Boulevard, you might buy some already ancient-seeming buttons and then go plunk down $3.95 at Licorice Pizza on the Strip for the triple-disc *Wings Over America* with its larger-than-life gatefold and many great songs, but you could never shake the feeling that you were a child of divorce.

"We approached the material as no 'real-time' Beatles fans ever could: We were completists and micro-analysts. We read the *All Together Now* discography and Roy Carr's LP-sized biography and argued over the merits of this or that phase—'They were kinda sick of being mop-tops by the time *Help!* happened, dude,' '*The White Album* signaled the demise, bro'—with the vigor and the rigor of junior historians.

"It is for this reason that John Lennon's murder was, for us, a double whammy. A vague and unconscious hope was finally silenced. History had spoken its piece, for all time, and the decade we missed— with its limitless dreams—would not be recovered."

**(Left to right) Dr. William Coleman, Joan Baez, John Lennon, Ira Sandperl, Benedict Canyon, California -- August 1965
Courtesy of Joanne Warfield**

ACKNOWLEDGMENTS:

Harvey Kubernik would like to thank the support received with some help from his friends: Andrew Solt, David Leaf, Marshall & Hilda Kubernik, Kenneth Kubernik, Candy Dog, Charlie Watts, Gary Strobl, Henry Diltz, Nancy Rose Retchin, Rodney Bingenheimer, Michele Myer, Cyril Jordan, Harold Sherrick, Steven J. Kalinich, Carol Schofield, Gary Stewart, David A. Barmack, Denny Bruce, Dr. James Cushing, Kim Fowley, Brad Elterman, Danny Weizmann, Paul Williams, Sherry Hendrick, Judy Pike, Tom Petty, Ron Lando, Greg Franco, Dean Dean - the Taping Machine, Dan Kessel, Little Steven, Joseph McCombs, Ritchie Yorke, Margot Gerber, Kirk Silsbee, Izzy Chait, Frank Orlando, Bob Sherman, Michael Hartman, Steven Gaydos, Jim Roup, Paul Body, Rosemarie Renee Patronette, Clem Burke, Jason Schwartzman, Tosh Berman, Richard Bosworth, Gary Pig Gold, George Schoenman, Lanny Waggoner, Roxanne Teti, Nick Roylance, Elliot Kendall, Ken Sharp, Gary Schneider at Open Mynd Collectibles, Ti, David Kessel, Royston Ellis, Chris Darrow, David Carr, Jimmy O'Neill, Mick Farren, Rob Hill, Lonn Friend, Matt King, Allan Rinde, Wanda Coleman, Micky Dolenz, Gia, Charlene Nowak, Norman Winter, Jeanne, Jennifer Ballantyne, Heather Harris, Roger Steffens, Justin Pierce, Cynthia Kirk, Jim Ladd, Les Perry, Bob Malick, Jim Carson, Kathie Zeigler, Biba Pickles, Paul Blair, Ray Coleman, Jeremy Gilien, Joel Selvin, Art Kunkin, Eva Leaf, Sid Bernstein, Jeff Goldman, Randy Haecker, Gia, Tina, Jim Kaplan, Roy Trakin, Chico Hamilton, Jim Keltner, Dr. David B. Wolfe, Riley, Book Soup, Mick Vranich, Amiri Baraka, Bob Say, Jeff Gold, Pooch, Tom Johnson, Phil Everly, Andrew Loog Oldham, Joe Meidlinger and Travis Edward Pike.

It Was 50 Years Ago Today: The Beatles Invade America and Hollywood

ABOUT THE AUTHOR

Harvey Kubernik
Photo: S. Ti Muntarbhorn

Los Angeles native Harvey Kubernik has been an active music journalist for over 40 years and the author of 5 books, including *This Is Rebel Music* (2002) and *Hollywood Shack Job: Rock Music In Film and on Your Screen* (2004) published by the University of New Mexico Press.

In 2009 Kubernik wrote the critically acclaimed *Canyon of Dreams: The Magic and the Music of Laurel Canyon*, published by Sterling. It was published in a paperback edition in 2012.

He is also a writer of *That Lucky Old Sun*, a Genesis Publications limited-edition (2009) title ($900.00 signed) done in collaboration with Brian Wilson of the Beach Boys and Sir Peter Blake, designer of the Beatles' *Sgt. Pepper's Lonely Hearts Club Band* album sleeve.

With his brother Kenneth, he co-authored the highly regarded *A Perfect Haze: The Illustrated History of the Monterey International Pop Festival*, published in 2011 by Santa Monica Press. They have also teamed up for a collaboration with photographer Guy Webster for Insight Editions, slated for late summer 2014.

For April 2014, Harvey Kubernik's *Turn Up the Radio! Rock, Pop and Roll in Los Angeles 1956-1972* book will be published by Santa Monica Press.

In fall of 2014, Palazzo Editions will publish *Leonard Cohen: Everybody Knows*, a coffee-table-size volume with narrative and oral history written by Harvey Kubernik.

His writings have been printed in several book anthologies, most notably *The Rolling Stone Book of the Beats* and *Drinking with Bukowski.*

This century Harvey penned the liner notes to the CD re-releases of Carole King's *Tapestry*, Allen Ginsberg's *Kaddish*, the *Elvis Presley '68 Comeback Special* and the Ramones' *End of the Century*. Kubernik currently serves as contributing editor of *Record Collector news,*

In 2013, Kubernik was seen on the BBC-TV documentary on Bobby Womack, *Across 110th Street,* directed by James Meycock and lensed for the spring 2014 Neil Norman–directed documentary about the Seeds.

Born at Queen of Angels Hospital in Echo Park, overlooking the Hollywood 101 Freeway, Harvey Kubernik first heard rock 'n' roll music in 1956 at the Coliseum Street and Muirfield Elementary Schools in the Crenshaw Village area and then later during El Marino Elementary School in Culver City. In January 1964, he eventually discovered the Beatles inside his parent's house in the Miracle Mile District.

A graduate of Fairfax High School and West Los Angeles College, he holds a B.A. Special Major Degree (Health, Sociology, Literature) from San Diego State University.

In November 2006, Kubernik was a featured speaker discussing audiotape preservation and archiving at special hearings called by The Library of Congress and held in Hollywood, California.

www.ingramcontent.com/pod-product-compliance
Lightning Source LLC
Chambersburg PA
CBHW070548160426
43199CB00014B/2420